OH, TO BE A FARMER!

Starting from the point of having no water in the house, and with only a wheelbarrow by way of farm equipment, this hilarious account of starting up in farming, in a remote part of upland Wales, covers some three years of the early 1950s. The difficulties and indignities suffered are offset by the marvellous sense of adventure and real living that underpin the story, to say nothing of the humorous idiosyncrasies of the neighbours and the intangible satisfaction that comes from working close to Nature.

OH, TO BE A FARMER!

OH, TO BE A FARMER!

by

Richard Barnett

Dales Large Print Books
Long Preston, North Yorkshire,
BD23 4ND, England.

British Library Cataloguing in Publication Data.

Barnett, Richard
    Oh, to be a farmer!

    A catalogue record of this book is
    available from the British Library

    ISBN   978-1-84262-660-3 pbl

First published in Great Britain in 1

Copyright © 1975 by Richard Barnet

Cover illustration © Dave Angel by arrangement with
britainonview

The moral right of the author has been asserted

Published in Large Print 2009 by arrangement with
Mr R. D. Barnett

Dales Large Print is an imprint of Library Magna Books Ltd.

Printed and bound in Great Britain by
T.J. (International) Ltd., Cornwall, PL28 8RW

To 'Bill', whose story this is, and whose sterling character, I like to think, shines through these pages.

Foreword

The events which I set down here for anyone who cares to read them took place in
the early 'fifties, soon after World War II. But
they remain so clearly imprinted in my
memory that I know I have only to 'keep my
head down' – an expression much used in
farming – for them to roll off my pen
without effort.

The adventure made such an impression
on my townsman's sensibilities that I believe
I have only to relate the story factually to
convey something of the fun, the satisfaction and the occasional anguish that the
experience gave me.

So, if you would care to leave your
comfortable armchair for a while and come
with me to the pretty uplands of mid-Wales,
I think I can promise to get some mud on
your boots.

Devon, Spring 1975

Contents

Chapter 1

Oh, to be a Farmer!

My brother, Bill, stands about 6'3" in his gumboots (size 12) and is remarkably well-developed across the chest and shoulders. He put more than one heavyweight to 'sleepybyes' in his college boxing days, and could throw a cricket ball further than anyone I ever knew.

Having been of school age during the greater part of the war, Bill spent most of his holidays on an uncle's farm in Herefordshire rather than suffer the shortages of life at our family home. The upshot was that he came to appreciate the country life from an early age and learned the skills of fishing, riding and shooting which were a closed book to the rest of us, so that long before he was fully grown he had decided irrevocably that farming was the life for him. He wasn't to know that he was witnessing a way of farming not destined to survive the war, based as it was on cheap labour, but he knew there was no other life to compare with it and he set his sights accordingly.

As things turned out, Bill's school days came to an end before the war did and he was to spend three years in the Army before he could turn his mind to the ways and means of achieving his ambition. No sooner was he out of uniform, however, than he started to prepare himself for it, first as a farm student with a leading dairy herd and, subsequently, at Agricultural College.

Although he realised only too well that substantial capital is a prerequisite of the farming world and unsure, as he was, about where it was going to come from, he never deviated for a moment from his single-minded purpose of striking out on his own as soon as his training was finished. Even the breathtaking figures of the farm economy books failed to put him off, and the fact that all his fellow students planned to take jobs in the farming world rather than attempt to go it alone, did nothing to alter his resolve.

Bill's hazy plan was to find a farm to rent, where he could make a start on the long haul of establishing a dairy herd, and play the thing by ear from there. The trouble was, as he came increasingly to realise, that farms to rent were exceedingly hard to find, thanks to the Security of Tenure Act which was so heavily loaded against the landlords. No sooner did a farm become vacant than the average owner would sell it rather than re-let under such unfavourable conditions, and only the really big estates seemed able to resist the pressure. But no agent would consider giving a tenancy to an impecunious beginner when he had any number of experienced farmers, still flush from their wartime profits clamouring for every farm that ever came up.

'There's nothing for it but to start at the very bottom,' I remember Bill saying, 'and that means, probably, a marginal hill farm in some wild part of Wales. Apparently they're so unprofitable that even the locals think twice about taking them on! Anyhow,' he said more than once, 'I don't care how hard I have to work, or how much I have to rough it, if only I can get my foot on the first rung of that farming ladder.' I was often to think of these words during the years that followed.

Now, it so happened that I was at a similar crossroads in life just then. Several years older than Bill, I was one of the 'elderly brigade' who went up to Cambridge after the war to be given degrees for two years' work instead of the usual three as some gesture of recognition of the interruption our education had suffered. I was slowly gravitating towards the teaching profession but reckoned I'd wasted enough of my life already and, if I was ever going to chance my arm the time to do it was surely ripe now that my university days were coming to an end.

Sometime during my last couple of terms I conceived the idea of joining up with brother Bill in a dual enterprise, first to get his farm established, however long that might take, and subsequently to use the established farm as a basis on which to build nothing less than a school of my own. Quite an ambitious scheme having regard to the limited funds we could put our fingers on at that time. But I knew that large houses, suitable for my purpose, were to be had for a song in those austerity-bound post-war years, and I believed I could find a place with the necessary acres when the time came. Truth to tell, my plans were as vague as Bill's, but the bare bones were clear enough and we both felt the scheme to be basically sound. We should just have to feel our way and take our chances as they came. Of course, for all I knew, we might never get beyond the first phase, the little matter of getting established in the farming world, but it all seemed eminently worthwhile and infinitely preferable to taking some safe job in the academic sphere as my tutors were urging me to do.

The fact that I scarcely knew an oak from an elm and that my experience of farming was limited to hay-making as a boy, a fun occupation that comprised hanging on to the backs of haycarts, riding on the massive shire horses and an occasional surreptitious swig at the cider jar, did nothing to put me off. I was more than happy to rely on Bill's farming know-how, having long admired his country skills. And as for the effort likely to be involved, that worried me not at all, for I was at an age when physical exertion is really a pleasure and the absence of comfort a laugh. Besides, I had recently felt an overpowering urge towards the simple life, as a reaction to the rule-bound existence that had been my lot through school, the Services and University, and the idea of a bit of basic living with nose to Mother Earth appealed enormously.

And so the die was cast. No sooner was Bill's final term at an end in early June than he set off for the Welsh outback, armed with a few introductions from his college friends and determined to find a farm to rent – or bust in the attempt. At much the same time my own term was coming to an end and I was charged with the vital job of finding some sort of a farm vehicle, perhaps an old shooting-brake, since we were clearly going to need something more than Bill's motor-bike.

Chapter 2

A Bit off the Beaten Track

In my day at Cambridge, when the place was full of people who had been right through the action, the so-called 'period of the Captains and Colonels', many of them nearer thirty than twenty, some married and some maimed, there was an intriguing selection of old 'bangers' jostling amongst the massed cyclists on Kings Parade. They ranged from baby Austins to elderly sports cars and even limousines belonging to an earlier age. These latter had, no doubt, been resurrected from cold storage when petrol came off the ration, but they somehow typified the idiosyncratic humour which did so much to give the place its atmosphere. Although I never ran to anything better than a rickety bicycle myself, I had often stopped to enjoy the incongruous sight of some humorist riding in a dickey-seat in full academic dress or, perhaps, half a dozen solemn-faced undergraduates driving past in an ancient tourer with umbrellas up against the weather. There was even one old limousine often seen crawling around the town at about half walking pace as a result of having suffered some irreparable damage to its vital parts, the owner and his friends taking it in turn to provide the motive power with their shoulders! At that time, cars of the twenties and early thirties had not become the collectors' pieces they are today, and there was precious little market for them outside the university; in consequence the principal expense lay in maintenance costs rather than initial outlay and, indeed, they changed hands quite cheaply whenever an owner found himself running low in funds.

It was not surprising therefore, that when my enquiries at garages and amongst the motoring fraternity brought me to the realisation that anything in the way of a shooting-brake was likely to set me back two or three hundred pounds, I began to consider the possibility of something in the 'old crock' line, not least because they intrigued me as vehicles in themselves. But, of course, we needed something capable of carrying all sorts of farm commodities, sacks and maybe even animals. Above all, it needed to be reliable, something the Cambridge 'bangers' most palpably were not. It wouldn't be much good if we had to get out and clean the plugs every few miles as my friend, Ian Trotter, had to do with his 1924 Sunbeam 'special'. And, judging from the number of people to be seen frantically swinging their vehicles along the highways and byways of the university precincts, the matter of easy starting was also something to be borne in mind.

'I've seen just the thing for you two madmen!' said Ian one day, after I'd spent a week or so pestering all my acquaintances for help in the search. 'There's a chap at Queen's with a fine old London taxi – you know, with folding hood at the back and open luggage space alongside the driver. The point is that it only came off the London streets about six months ago, and it's in really good nick mechanically as they have to be maintained to a very high standard to meet the Metropolitan Police tests. There's stacks of room in the back, especially with the seats out and the hood down, and think how useful that luggage platform would be for sacks and things!'

'Hmm... And what sort of money does he want for it?'

'Eighty quid, I believe. And I doubt if you'd get a better vehicle at three times the price.'

Eighty quid! That was really talking! And a reliable old bus to boot – it sounded too good to be true and I wasted no time in getting Ian to take me round to see it.

To say that I immediately fell for the comical-looking old car hook, line and sinker, would be to understate the case. For all the world like something out of an Emett drawing, it looked Edwardian to my un-tutored eye, the sort of thing that followed on immediately from the open carriages of the earliest days of motoring. A genuine black bulb-hooter projected from the driver's side of the windscreen and the heavy leather hood at the back was folded down, cabriolet fash-ion, to expose the rear seat. At once dignified and comical, it combined the exaggerated height and ornamental finish of a bygone age with obvious utilitarian design. Everything from the tyres to the rich red leather up-holstery appeared unmarked and the whole effect was capped with an impressive monogram on each of the doors.

'She's a 1934 Austin,' explained the owner, opening the bonnet, 'four cylinder, twelve horse and the engine's as good as ever. In fact, the only mechanical fault she has is a noisy cog in bottom gear and that's nothing to worry about.'

'And what sort of m.p.g. do you get?'

'A bit heavy, certainly – about twenty on a decent run, I'd say, but she uses no oil which is more important in an old car. All the usual wear-spots, kingpins, transmission and so on, have been replaced and, as you can see, there's no rust anywhere.'

He gave a half-turn on the starting handle and the engine sprang to life. Ian cupped a hand over the exhaust in professional fashion and nodded his approval before we clambered in for a spin round the Backs, with me squatting on the luggage platform alongside the driver and Ian peering through the little sliding window behind us. But long before we got back to base I had decided to buy and my own turn at the wheel was merely a formality.

It only remained to clinch the deal, and I was soon bumbling along behind Ian on the way back to our college, thrilled to bits with my new acquisition and chortling at its likely impact on Bill and the staid folk of Welsh Wales. That same evening I got a 'phone call from Shrewsbury.

'I've found a farm, mun!' came Bill's voice, in his humorous way.

'Have you really? Well done, indeed! Somewhere near Shrewsbury?'

'No, not really, but roughly on the same latitude, I suppose. A bit off the beaten track, you might say – fifteen miles to be exact.'

'I don't call that too bad, fifteen miles from Shrewsbury. Quite nice land, I should think, near the Welsh border.'

'No, fifteen miles from the nearest market town.'

'Oh!'

'But there's a village a mile or two down the road, so we won't starve.'

'Hmm! Well, what's the name of the town, then?'

'The countryside is breathtaking and the view is worth more than the rent,' hedged Bill.

'It sounds as if it's halfway up Cader Idris!'

'Well, it's somewhere near Lake Vyrnwy – if that means anything to you. It's a marginal hill farm really, on the side of a little valley, but there are several reasonable fields for dairying and the buildings are ideal.'

'And how about the house?'

'Oh, it's a fascinating house,' returned Bill with what sounded suspiciously like a hollow laugh. 'Just wait till you see it! Not much in the way of mod. cons. of course, but very picturesque. It's what they call a Welsh "longhouse", very old with cowshed built on to one end and giving a long, low effect. Anyhow, how are you getting on with organising that shooting-brake?'

'It's all fixed! Not exactly a shooting-brake but the next best thing. And it only cost eighty quid.'

'That's marvellous! How on earth did you manage it? What sort of car is it, then?'

'Well, it's a convertible really. You know with a hood and all that. Bags of room in the back, too. Just you wait till you see it!' This time the hollow laugh was mine.

'How soon can you come on up with it?' Bill went on. 'The place is empty, so I've decided to move in early next week. There's a devil of a lot to be done before we can get any animals, so the sooner we can start the better.'

'I should be able to get away from here by about Wednesday, but I'll have to take all my stuff home first, of course.'

'O.K. I'll let you have a list of things to

bring with you, and directions to find the place, and I'll hope to see you before the week is out.'

So we were off! I could scarcely believe my good fortune after so many years of institutional restrictions. To throw off the shackles and escape to the countryside, with no one to breathe down our necks and with no stupid superiors to be beholden to, where we would sink or swim according to our own efforts, seemed the fulfilment of some secret longing and I could scarcely wait to get started.

Look out, Farming, here we come!

Chapter 3

Not Much in the Way of Mod. Cons.

Thanks to my stylish new mode of transport, I seemed to have a lot more friends than hitherto during that final week or so at University. Blokes I had always passed on the stairs with never so much as a friendly nod, suddenly seemed to see the error of their ways and almost fell over one another in their efforts to ingratiate themselves. But my new-found popularity could only last till the time came to load up all the books and other possessions collected in my time 'up', before finally heading out of Cambridge towards what I felt instinctively would be some Real Living after years of artificiality.

Something of a circuitous route was called for to reach my parents' home in Sussex without having to chance my arm in the heart of London, but I made it safely to enjoy the laughter and approval of our neighbours before loading up the old car once more for the long trip to the land of the Celt.

I was soon bumbling along the open road once more, this time heading west with Worcester my first milestone and a sense of adventure bubbling up inside me. Fortunately, it was a fine summer's day and the old vehicle made good time on the near-empty roads. Apart from the stares of passers-by, which I was slowly getting accustomed to, the only trouble was a tendency to stall the engine at traffic lights and level crossings. More than once I was obliged to hop out of the cab smartly to crank the starting-handle while holding up a line of traffic, but the other motorists showed only amusement, especially when the handle flew round backwards, as occasionally happened, to my discomfiture.

I reached the Welsh border beyond Ludlow by mid-afternoon, purring along at about forty miles an hour, this being the old cab's cruising speed which she could only better when free-wheeling down steep slopes. Great mountain bluffs began to loom ominously but the weather held and before very long I was well and truly into Welsh Wales. The scenery had become quite picturesque with its undulating patchwork of small fields against the impressive mountainous sweeps of the background. More and more stops were called for to ponder the map as the roads became narrower and steeper, but by early evening I had dropped down a steep scarp to give the little village of Tresiliog its first glimpse of a genuine old London taxi.

I was faintly disappointed to see no tall Welsh hats or shawls in evidence but had no difficulty in following Bill's directions along the little valley until I found the lane I wanted on the right-hand side. 'Vendre Fach', scrawled in black paint on an old piece of board near the entrance, clinched the matter, and I swung the taxi straight in. I can't pretend that she made light of that lane, for all her good springing, either then or on any subsequent occasion, for the potholes were pretty liberally dotted about and it was impossible to avoid them all. Nevertheless, after a few hundred jolting yards, a pretty little farmhouse hove into view, whitewashed and quaint in its setting of woods and green fields, and I drew up before it with great aplomb and loud honking of the bulb-hooter.

Bill's massive form soon emerged from one of the outbuildings and he was beside himself with admiration for the old car.

'And only eighty quid – that's the best of it!' he chortled. 'Let's have a dekko at the engine. Hmm ... well, I'm blowed, she sounds perfect. Just what we need, I reckon!'

'So this is Vendre Fach!' I said, approvingly, when the car inspection was finished. 'And how's it going?'

'I've made a start on organising some water in the house,' returned Bill, 'but it's a big job burying the polythene pipe and I hope you're feeling fit for a spot of trench digging?'

'Do you mean to say there's no water in the house?' I gasped.

'Good heavens, no! There's an excellent spring up there above the barn, though, and the locals say it never dries up, so we're lucky. That's where I'm leading the pipe from, of course. Come and have a look.'

Sure enough, from a large cleft of rock cutting back into the steep field above it, was pouring a steady little torrent, cleverly channelled into an old wooden barrel. So this was all our predecessors had had in the way of mod cons. I began to realise just how primitive things were at Vendre. We really were starting from scratch, it seemed.

'Come and see where you're sleeping,' said Bill, leading me back down to the cottage and through the low front door. The 'bedroom' was a long, low attic with all the roof beams wide open to view, complete with huge wooden nails at the principal intersections. The only light came from two extraordinarily low windows, at front and rear of the house, set into the tops of the walls and hardly reaching eighteen inches above the level of the floor. To look out of them you needed to get down on hands and knees, and they could only be opened by lifting out the entire frames. Two mattresses were lying on the floor with blankets churned up on one to show where Bill had slept.

'I'm glad you've brought some bedding with you,' he laughed. 'The landlord's wife lent me this stuff and I don't want to ruin it.

She says we can keep the mattresses, though.'

Downstairs was mainly taken up by a large kitchen, but there was also a tiny front parlour, a small dairy near the back door and one or two other closets which were to prove useful as time went on. The most striking feature of the kitchen, apart from the lingering smell of wood smoke, was the enormous fireplace and chimney, taking up almost the full width of the room.

'Just take a look up here,' laughed Bill, standing his large bulk comfortably upright in the chimney place. 'I'm blessed if I see how the fire can draw properly with such a wide flue, but I haven't tried it yet.'

There was no doubt at all that it had worked well in the past, for everything there – old fashioned oven, heavy chain for holding the kettle and all the brickwork – was thickly coated with shiny, black wood soot. There was no sink of any sort nor, of course, any water tap to go with it. The yard-wide windowsills showed the extraordinary thickness of the walls, themselves clearly in need of attention with the paper torn in places and loose plaster falling from the tears. The low ceiling, supported by two massive oak beams, was made up of wooden joists a foot or so apart and supporting the floorboards of the 'bedroom' above. Unfortunately, all the beams and joists had been papered over and painted a horrid mud colour. As for furniture, there was simply a kitchen table and a couple of hard chairs lent by the landlord's wife until we could get some stuff of our own. The only sign of the times was a little two-ring gas stove, complete with grill, which Bill had found in Welshpool and had installed with a large cylinder of gas. This was to prove invaluable as time went by.

'And how am I going to cook the joint and two veg I've had such careful instructions about – not to mention Grandma's fruit cake?' I inquired.

'I don't think that old oven in the grate will be much use to us, so we'll have to get one of those oil burner things,' returned Bill. 'They're quite cheap and, now we've got the car, I can get one up here easily enough.'

He boiled a saucepan of water on the gas-ring and we shared the first of many a life-saving pot of tea together, augmented by some cake I'd been furnished with before leaving home. Afterwards I was taken on a tour of the farm in the evening sunshine. Nestling on the side of the steep little valley, the farmstead seemed to me quite idyllic at that moment and I felt instinctively that I was going to love the place. And when, eventually, I turned in on my mattress alongside Bill to dream of fun and fresh air, it was with the rare conviction that Fate was smiling for once in a way and that the little farm was going to match up to all my hopes of it.

Roll on tomorrow!

Chapter 4

First Crop of Blisters

We were up in good time next morning to a refreshing wash in the old barrel at the spring, a pleasant little early morning routine which was to last till we had achieved our first mod. con. in laying on the water to the house. On the principle of starting as we intended to continue, we ate a huge breakfast of bacon and eggs, fried potatoes, fried bread and fried tomatoes, soon to be augmented by mushrooms which abounded in the bottom meadow. One of the principal pleasures of farming, I was soon to learn, lies in the satisfying of ravenous hunger. The work outdoors gives one an appetite far beyond one's norm and, if one is to keep going at all, it must be satisfied. So we made a point of eating well, and food was one thing we never skimped on.

Bill's plan was to get the place shipshape before the first animals arrived in about three weeks' time, when half a dozen cows from the landlord's herd were due to come to us. The old boy was letting us have them at the reasonable price of thirty pounds a head as he would have to reduce his herd to compensate for the acres being handed over to us. Bill had ostensibly taken over on the June quarter day and the date fixed for the handover of the cows was July 15th.

There were three main tasks to be tackled in those few weeks, top priority being the installing of running water, while the old cowshed had to be brought up to standard for TT milk production, and the kitchen-cum-living room clearly needed a face-lift. Obviously we were going to have our work cut out to do it in the time available, but we well knew that time for such jobs would be hard to find once we had stock to look after, so we pitched in with a will.

The work with the pickaxe, burying the plastic water pipe, produced my first crop of blisters but, even so, that basic task of bringing water to the house proved to be one of the most satisfying jobs I ever remember doing. Perhaps the best of it was that we were tapping our own little water supply and a simple spring of untreated water at that; no mains, no reservoir, not even a well was involved. The transformation we had achieved when, finally the pipe had been laid, the yard-thick wall of the kitchen breached, the gleaming new sink installed and we had only to turn a tap in order to draw on the little spring way up beyond the hay barn, seemed almost magical. In some strange way it did my soul more good to complete that task than a hundred more complex ones.

More important in Bill's book, if not in mine, was the branch pipe to the cowshed and dairy without which we would not qualify for a milk producer's licence. But there was something else the cowshed needed: nothing less than the refacing of all its interior walls with a smooth cement finish, capable of regular scrubbing. I, consequently became a human cement-mixer for several days at a stretch while Bill applied my produce to the walls by the hundredweight. Mercifully, the rules required the cement finish to a height of six feet only, but it proved a huge task even so.

'I never want to see another bag of cement!' I gasped, when the final barrow-load had gone on. 'I must have mixed about three tons all told. What a job!'

'I've got a nasty feeling the kitchen walls are going to call for the same treatment,' returned Bill, cheerfully. 'The plaster is quite hollow in places and the paper's about the only thing holding it up, I reckon. Let's go and see the worst.'

The paper was certainly pretty tatty and, where it was already peeling, we had no option but to remove it. As we did so, some alarmingly large chunks of plaster came with it to confirm Bill's fears. We soon realised, though, that it wasn't really plaster behind the paper, but a build-up, over the centuries, of successive coats of whitewash, alternating with the pink variety. Before we quite appreciated what we were letting ourselves in for, we had gone beyond the point of no return, and were faced with the major operation of removing the 'plaster' right down to the solid wall some three or four inches behind, and re-plastering completely.

My heart sank as I took in the extent of the cementing job we were heading for, and I hate to think how much dust we inhaled as the crumbling old layers of wash were hacked off to reach the first-sized pebbles which made up the inner surface of the massive walls.

But this time Bill and I took it in turns to mix the stuff, for no great skill was called for in slapping it on, at least in the early stages when the object was simply to bury the undulating pebbles, however roughly. And by the time we had applied enough cement to achieve a reasonably flat surface, I had gained sufficient experience to keep my end up without spoiling the effect. We made no attempt to finish off with plaster, but simply mixed the cement as finely as we could in the later stages in order to get a reasonably smooth finish. The waves and bulges were so pronounced, anyway, that a small matter like a proper finish seemed pointless.

Since the kitchen was going to be our living-room we went to a lot of trouble to make a good job of it, not only giving it new walls but resurrecting the fine oak beams and joists by scraping off the horrid brown paint and paper, prior to creosoting them for a good black finish and whitening the dirty strips of ceiling in between. Finally we painted the walls an attractive shade of light green and we had transformed the place.

While all this was going on we 'pigged it' amongst the rubble. Fortunately, it was high summer and we were new to the rustic life, so it was all a bit of a laugh at that early stage.

Before our three weeks' grace was up, a load of family furniture arrived, so that we now had real beds to sleep in, cupboards for the food and even a carpet on the flag-stoned kitchen floor, something it could hardly have known before. Bill duly bought the oil burner to augment our two gas-rings and grill, and it wasn't long before he went bust on a smart new sanitary closet as an improvement on the outdoor model across the vegetable garden, generally know as 'Ty Bach' (Little House). We christened our more modern device the 'Johann Sebastian' in recognition of our mutual distaste for the great Welsh composer, as he's sometimes called, and installed it in a tiny annex which adjoined the front parlour, something of an embarrassment when, in the fullness of time, we had guests.

As for a bath, Bill soon found a galvanised zinc model at an ironmonger's in Newtown, and we were able to enjoy the dubious pleasure of bathing in front of the kitchen fire. I would like to put on record my hearty distaste for this time-honoured method of bathing, as much for the discomfort of the near-vertical sides as for the gale force draughts in front of our particular kitchen fire, to say nothing of the business of emptying it afterwards. Add to all that the difficulties we faced in heating sufficient water in kettles and saucepans and it wasn't surprising that our life-long bathing habits quickly deteriorated well beyond the old joke about Friday night being Bath Night. Lady Day and Michaelmas would have been nearer the mark!

Chapter 5

Pig Passengers

The first farm task the old taxi, still resplendent in its monogrammed doors, was called upon to perform was to take Elsie the sow on a visit to the boar, a quite horrific character who resided near Caersws, about fifteen miles away over an awful mountain road. The problem was how to get Elsie's great bulk up the step into the car, and Bill decided to coax her with a bucket of swill till her front feet were on the running board, when he would grab her ears while I shoved with all I'd got from the rear.

'I expect she'll go in a treat!' said Bill.

Having taken out all the removable leather seats and made sure the hood was firmly fastened in the closed position, we let Elsie out from her sty and Bill led her easily enough to the car door with his bucket of swill. I took up my station in the rear as stealthily as I could, thankful to have the less dangerous end of proceedings but a bit apprehensive nevertheless as the huge animal gingerly mounted the running board in order to keep her head in the bucket.

'Right – SHOVE!' yelled Bill, grabbing her great ears while I applied my shoulder in best rugger-scrum fashion from behind. But somehow Elsie's legs caught in the running board and the whole thing went awry. She knocked the bucket flying and fled across the yard with frightful screams.

'Blast the old devil!' puffed Bill. 'We'll have to think of a better scheme than that.'

'Well, as long as you don't want me on the front end…' I countered.

'I was thinking that if you were to take the bucket…'

'Oh, no…'

'…and coax her actually head and shoulders inside the car…'

'Not on your life, thanks!'

'You don't have to grab hold of her, or anything, and once her front half is inside I'll be able to shove her in easily from the rear.'

'Wonderful idea! So I'm in the car with the enraged sow?'

'You'll have to get out smartish from the other door, you clot!'

I had nasty visions of being trodden underfoot at the crucial moment or perhaps partaken of as an extra titbit, but I was eventually persuaded to risk my all.

So we tried again. Only Elsie's insatiable appetite enabled us to get her to the car a second time, as her suspicions were now very much aroused and she was squealing with fright even while grabbing great mouthfuls from the bucket. To my surprise she followed me right into the car, as planned, until her front end was well and truly inside. I had taken the precaution of leaving the opposite door ajar and scarcely waited for Bill's shout as he grabbed Elsie's back legs and threw them in. Both doors were slammed instantaneously and we were enjoying a good laugh together while Elsie wondered what had hit her.

'Bloody good effort!' I cheeped excitedly. 'I never thought she'd fall for it like that, I must say.'

'I hope she doesn't go on the rampage now we've got her in – better get going to keep her mind occupied!' returned Bill, clambering into the driver's seat.

But the fun was by no means at an end when the sow was safely aboard. Ominous sounds of ripping upholstery tended to punctuate the drive to Caersws, and a bucket of apples or potatoes was a 'must' at the driver's side for throwing in on these occasions. Sometimes the whole car would lurch alarmingly as the huge animal indulged in some odd gyrations or lost its balance on a corner. But the thing that remains most vividly in my mind about these trips is the breathtaking close-up view of the sow's dental equipment when she occasionally thrust her great face through the communicating window about three inches from my left ear. Fortunately the gap was sufficient only for the jaws to come through, the head itself being too wide.

'Down, Elsie, DOWN!' I'd bawl, trying to make my meaning clearer with frantic

41

waving, at the same time lobbing an apple or two through the window and trying not to forget entirely that I was steering with the other hand.

On one of these trips – with Gertie, I remember, the more excitable of the sisters – the old taxi started boiling and emitting an alarming amount of steam on one of the many frightful hills. The faces of the woman and her children, at whose house I stopped for some water, were quite something to behold when they came out to watch proceedings. Gertie was having one of her face-through-the-window turns to add to the astonishment shown by these country people at the sight of a pig in what they took to be a hearse.

The smell emanating from the pig farm was so powerful that one could almost home in on it for the last five miles or so, and was usually greeted on arrival by the proprietor himself. 'Greeted' is hardly the right word, however, for Mr Rhys, a wizened little man in his sixties, was not much given to the niceties of social convention. Indeed, he seemed to have taken on the cunning looks and general contour of face of his charges over the years, and become almost one of them. Undoubtedly he could have bought us out fifty times over, being the best-known pig breeder in the district, but he showed no sign of having progressed in other respects from the lowest type of farm hand.

'Good afternoon!' I ventured, drawing up sedately with my passenger on my first visit. 'My brother 'phoned you yesterday, I believe?'

'Grunt!' said Mr Rhys, in charming fashion.

'Where do you want her to go?'

'Grunt! Grunt!' he replied, evidently reluctant to be too chatty but, to my surprise, opening the door to let Gertie out in the forecourt where we stood.

A good quarter of an hour then ensued trying to persuade Gertie to go through an open gate into an inner yard. First she would tear off to the right, screaming at Rhys's efforts to head her off with a stick, then the other way at a rate of knots, carefully bypassing the open gate each time until I, at least, felt like giving it up as a bad job. Some of Mr Rhys's grunts bore a strong resemblance to oaths at this point, but he certainly showed himself a remarkable sprinter for his age.

'The grunting Grunt!' he wheezed heavily, as we finally got her through the gate at the twenty-fifth attempt. I never could understand how experienced pig men would leave so much to chance, knowing so well their charges' instinct to go every way but the right one. But I had to admire their pertinacity.

Chapter 6

Founder-member Livestock

By the second week in July, with the arrival of our livestock imminent, we had achieved a good deal in the way of preparation. The cowshed and little dairy were duly inspected by an official from the Ministry who expressed the pious hope that we would keep them as clean as they were then at all times, adding rather ominously that he was liable to look in at any time, 'to see we were all right', as he put it.

The kitchen, in practice the living-room, dining-room, study, pantry, reception room and occasional bathroom, had been transformed into a most attractive oak-beamed room of olde worlde style, and our landlord's charming and capable wife, who did a great deal to help us get settled in, was full of

44

approval for our efforts. She not only worked around the clock herself, having a substantial poultry enterprise to look after single-handed, quite apart from running a big house with hardly any staff, but found time to make us a weekly cake and to pop over regularly to see what we needed. She lent us any amount of stuff to tide us over until our own furniture arrived and was tireless in getting things we needed on her visits to town.

As things turned out, the first livestock we acquired were not cows at all, but pigs. Bill's first joust with Newtown market resulted in two fine Large White sows complete with litters, eight or nine funny little piglets each. The pig breed known as 'Large White' is most assuredly large if not often white, except when scrubbed with a view to sale in the market. It is the largeness part which strikes the townsman so forcibly when first confronted with these animals at close range, and so it was when Bill asked me to join him in the lorry to help push out our two newcomers, who seemed reluctant to descend the ramp on the day they arrived.

'Don't you think it would be better to coax them out with some food?' I suggested, hopefully.

'No, come on! They'll be out in a trice

with the two of us. They're very friendly!' added Bill, sensing my lack of enthusiasm.

Getting close to those enormous jaws was something I never did feel too happy about but, strangely enough, although she can rip a heavy rubber tyre to shreds like so much paper, the sow never seems tempted to use her frightful mouth on her human persecutors. Invariably she will turn and flee with a mixture of squeals and grunts.

'The chap who sold them told me they're sisters,' explained Bill when we had eventually got them installed in their respective sties. 'This one's Elsie and the other's called Gertie. These are only their first litters, so there should be plenty more in store.'

I was intrigued with the piglets, never having seen such little ones before. They have none of their mother's oafishness and it is hard to believe they are her progeny, really. Their bright little faces, quizzical expressions, twiddling tails and quick dashes in all directions are fascinating to watch. But, as Bill remarked about a later batch, it is a wonder they don't all die of shock when they see what they've got for a mother!

Mother, though, is far from stupid. Although weighing about a fifth of a ton as against the two or three pounds of her new-born babes, she can usually manage to lay her great bulk down without squashing or suffocating any of her brood, and she keeps the inside of her home as clean as the proverbial whistle. She enjoys her food certainly, and is somewhat noisy in partaking thereof, but in most respects she belies the unfortunate appearance Nature has given her.

One of the pleasures of farming is that when you're enjoying some particular aspect, such as in this case simply watching the antics of piglets, you don't have to break away to get on with something else or to catch a train. You may spend ten minutes or more just savouring whatever it is that has caught your eye, knowing that the next job can wait. It's almost impossible to estimate the time required for farm jobs – I soon learnt that a farmer's five minutes is rarely less than half an hour – so time is not often pressing and one simply goes to bed a bit later if it gets in short supply.

Within a few days of our becoming pig breeders, we reached the first rung of the main ladder and became dairy farmers, when six cows from the landlord's herd of Ayrshires were duly driven over and the old man came to see the hand-over.

'There w'are, there w'are, old boy. The

best of my herd, really. Very sorry to see them go, but such is life, eh? Damn fine cows, old boy. Damn fine cows!' And while we took this with the large pinch of salt it deserved, the fact was that at least three of the six proved to be excellent milkers and contributed largely to the establishment of our own herd with their daughters over the years.

The Ayrshire cow is a hardy breed, most often brown and white and of rather dainty physique, lacking the beefier qualities of breeds such as the Friesian but with fine, upstanding horns that give it a handsome appearance all its own. Nowadays most calves are deprived of their horn 'buds' soon after birth and horned cattle have become something of a rarity, much to the detriment of their looks, but it had not become the general practice at that time and all the cattle we ever had at Vendre were horned.

Probably the best of the bunch was a small cow called Hyacinth who could be relied upon to keep milking right through each lactation instead of going 'dry' as most cows do sooner or later. I was amazed to find that a good cow will give upwards of five *gallons* of milk a day in the early stages after calving and may still be giving three gallons halfway through her lactation; indeed, it is a cow's capacity to maintain a substantial production for many months, rather than to give an impressive amount at the start only to dwindle rapidly in the later stages, that the farmer looks for. But, as I was soon to discover, the business of extracting all this liquid can prove a tough job. It is all right with a quiet cow like Hyacinth, who 'lets her milk down' properly and is generally easy to milk, but the majority have some awkward quirk. They seem to put the brakes on and resist in one way or another, calling for real effort on the part of the poor chap on the stool to achieve so much as a dribble.

I came to love our cows, beautiful animals and generally so docile. Why the townsman should think of them as gormless creatures is beyond me, for they have an endless range of character and I never found any two really alike. I always felt that dairy farming is superior to most other forms of animal husbandry where the slaughterhouse is the awful destination, usually at the animals' prime of life. Old dairy cows, of course, have to go the same way eventually, but until they start to fail they are looked after with loving care by the farmer, whose livelihood depends on keeping them fit and well nourished. Roll on the day when mankind can do without meat!

Our founder-member livestock was completed by fifty golden Leghorns, many of which were given individual names in the course of time, a tiny tabby kitten which was to do stout work around our feed bins, and a fine black Labrador pup called Trigger. We were all set to become an established farm – or so we thought.

Chapter 7

Colourful Neighbours

Our nearest neighbours were, like ourselves, tenants of Capt. Lloyd-Vaughan's Craig-y-bryn estate. Gareth Price was a fine young Welshman whose family had farmed Bryn-coed for generations and, as a result, he knew the strengths and weaknesses of our fields almost as well as he knew his own. He and his buxom wife, Eirwen, proved the best of neighbours to us and, although their farm equipment ran only to a horse and cart as opposed to our wheelbarrows, they came to our rescue in many a crisis. Not that Gareth had much need of any machinery when he had a wife like Eirwen, a daughter of the soil if ever I saw one. Despite a brood of small kids, she was usually to be seen working out of doors, and often held the fort single-handed when Gareth was off helping on some neighbouring farm. She didn't bat an eyelid at humping heavy bags on her back, and could turn hay with a pitchfork better than any man I remember, going through a field of wet grass and flinging it in all directions like an old-fashioned 'tedder' machine. More than once Bill and I were astonished to see them get in a field of hay when there weren't two dry days together, while ours remained out getting blacker and blacker.

Eirwen had a laugh like the proverbial peal of bells, and it could often be heard echoing across the little valley. Her nature, adequately supported by her powerful physique, was to make light of all difficulties and to pitch in with a will to whatever was in the offing, however daunting it may have been to most people.

'I can't quite decide whether to get a Fordson or a Massey Harris!' Gareth used to say at regular intervals. He still hadn't quite decided by the time we left the district some three years later. Like most farmers in those parts, he preferred to run his finances without the aid of the banks, and we suspected the truth to be that the old sock under the bed would never quite run to it. But the horse and cart served them pretty well and no doubt Gareth needed his daydreams like the rest of us. We were to see a great deal of these two as time went on and I often wonder how we would have managed without their generous help.

A little further down the road, beyond Bryncoed, there dwelt another farmer we were to see a lot of. This was a middle-aged Latvian called Kropje, a displaced person with a sad background of having lost his family estates, first to the Russians and then to the Germans. Such, at least, was his story, but how much was authentic was difficult to judge, for Kropje was given to the old trouble of line-shooting, a failing that did little to endear him to the rather suspicious locals. Undoubtedly he had lost everything in the war and was now struggling with a farm even worse than ours in some respects, and with the added disadvantage of being an obvious foreigner, no easy thing to get away with amongst the Welsh who tend to find even the English pretty borderline. I always got on fairly well with this fellow – perhaps because of my wide-eyed innocence in farming matters – but he soon got under Bill's skin with his know-all manner, based as it was on a mixture of folklore and farming myths, very alien to Bill's scientific training. Even my credulity baulked, however, at the miraculous ability he claimed to have of being able to forecast the weather several seasons ahead.

'Is easy ven you know ze signs!' he often said, to Bill's annoyance. 'Ven ze chickens roost early, veel be a vet summer,' and other potty statements in the same vein, did little to endear him to people who had learnt to take their chances with the wireless forecasts.

I first met Kropje when he called one morning on his bicycle to arrange a lift into town. He boasted several items of farm equipment, albeit of the horse age, which Bill was keen to borrow, so quite a lot of back-scratching took place between the two. I gathered from the conversation that, notwithstanding his knowing all there was to know about farming, things were not going too well just then, for rabbits had decimated his field of oats, his potatoes seemed to have the blight and his best cow was down with mastitis.

'Veel be better next year!' he proclaimed

53

with an assurance which Bill and I could only put down to the clairvoyance which contributed so much to his farming technique.

'Did you notice my new milk stand?' inquired Bill of his fine piece of handiwork just completed at the end of our lane. I had been full of admiration for it when he showed it me a day or two before, for he had quite excelled himself in making a really stout job out of some old railway sleepers.

'Oh, yas. I see it,' returned Kropje, unenthusiastically. 'Veel do! Veel do!'

'Will do? I like that, don't you?' snorted Bill when Kropje had taken himself off back up the lane. 'You should see his moth-eaten affair – the struts are so weak he's tied it to the hedge with binder twine to stop it falling into the road! I'll give him "Will do".'

Evans-the-Road, as our local council workman was known to everyone, was very much of the old breed, a marvellous worker who took a pride in keeping his stretch of road really shipshape at all seasons. He was also an inveterate storyteller such as I imagine must have been before the days of universal literacy. The strange thing was that his anecdotes were so intensely interesting and, however pressed you were for time, he held you spellbound. Many a time I would be doing some job in a field near the road when his weather-beaten face would loom up over the hedge to provide a welcome diversion.

'It puts me in mind of the time...' he'd start, and away he would go on some tale of his younger days. It seems he was a 'mower' in his youth, one of a group of a dozen or so who would scythe the meadows in a line before the days of the cutter mower machine – and that is going back a bit. Naturally the weather prospects, always hazardous in upland Wales, were the most vital consideration before any mowing could begin, and the plan, he explained, was to start on his local squire's extensive hay meadows, somewhere down the valley towards Llanfair, on the morrow. All weather signs had been right for several days past and the mowers had honed their blades to a wonderful pitch in preparation for the early start next morning. Everyone was up at about four o'clock, full of excited anticipation at the prospect of starting another year's harvesting and, with the sun just risen, they emerged from the farmhouse to savour the promise of another beautiful day.

It was at this point that Evans heard the ominous words which were the crux of the story: 'Bugger it! Bugger it! Bugger it! Duffryn Conin's in the yard!' Evans repeated the phrase with relish once or twice as my expression denoted something less than full comprehension. It seemed that Duffryn Conin was the name of a farm way off on the hillside, about three miles from where they stood, and there it was looking so clear it might almost have been in their own yard!

Whether this well-known sign of rain put paid to the mowing I cannot recall, but the apt phrase became part of our farming vocabulary from that day on. Evans proved to be a stalwart of the district, welcome as much for his shrewd advice on farming matters as for his diverting yarns, and we came to know him well as time went on.

The village shop-cum-Post Office in Tresiliog was run by a delightful old character known for miles around as 'Uncle', in consequence, I gathered, of his having been the only boy in a large family of girls now settled in the neighbourhood. Uncle was not only shopkeeper and postmaster but banker, vet, doctor and priest rolled into one, partly on the strength of the wide range of goods he sold and partly because of his wise and kindly nature. I first met up with him when I hurried down to the village one Saturday soon after my arrival, with some urgent letters for the post. I arrived a full quarter of an hour before the advertised collection time only to be informed by Uncle, in a matter-of-fact tone, that it had already gone.

'But it's only half past four and the time on the box is four forty-five!' I remonstrated.

'Yes, yes,' said Uncle, unrepentant, 'but he'll be here again on Monday, whatever!' That seemed to square the matter as far as he was concerned.

The shop was very dark and in no way lumbered with food cases or anything superfluous of that sort. Pieces of cheese and bacon were left lying about on the counter so that customers could feel as well as see their quality. On one occasion, I remember, Uncle calmly cut out a maggoty piece from the bacon before slicing a few rashers for my order.

'Drat these old maggots!' was his only remark.

Questions such as 'What sort of cheese have you got today?' were not comprehended by Uncle who either had 'cheese' or 'no cheese'. You had to realise you were fortunate to get the commodity you required without wasting time on brand name or variety.

Another of our principal neighbours was one Watkyn Roberts, a comical little sixty-five-year old who ran a small engineering business with his son, Emrys, in Tresiliog. They dabbled between them in all sorts of engines, pumps and milking machines which were beginning to catch on with those who could afford the outlay. They also ran a lucrative sideline as occasional undertakers, and Watkyn was sometimes to be seen setting out in his ancient hearse, transformed from his usual scruffy appearance with top hat and all the trimmings. But for the most part he was hammering away at something in his junk-littered yard, or off at some neighbouring farm dealing with mechanical problems. Between them Roberts and Son looked after every mechanical contrivance within a radius of a dozen miles of the village and they were happy to come to the rescue at any time of the day or night.

Early on in our acquaintance we discovered that Watkyn, despite his lack of inches, was a man who wore the trousers with a vengeance in his household. Bill had gone to see him about some problem and was discussing it in casual fashion, sitting on an old trailer in the corner of Watkyn's yard. Suddenly, the little granddaughter came running out of the house.

'Grand-dad, come quick, Mam says. The tap in the kitchen is stuck and she can't turn it off!'

'Now, run away, Gladys, there's a good girl. You can see I'm busy,' said Watkyn, reverting to his chat with Bill quite unconcernedly.

Shortly afterwards the little girl reappeared, rather distraught.

'Grand-dad, Mam says if you don't come quick the kitchen will be flooded! She can't stop the tap.'

'Now, leave me alone, Gladys, like I told you. Go on, 'op it quick!' snapped Watkyn, with some vehemence, whereupon she burst into tears and retired once more.

The third time the child came back, near hysterical, with dire news of flooding and carpets being ruined, Watkyn's patience finally snapped.

'If you don't bugger off, child, once and for all, I'll put the stick across your arse!'

In due course we met up with all the neighbours. Sincerity was their common denominator and they were neighbourly in the true sense of the word. It may well have been because of the tough lives they led in wresting a subsistence from their holdings, but we came to feel that these people were more genuine than most. Certainly, when we eventually moved farm to richer pastures, we noticed a striking difference for the worse amongst the more affluent farmers who had made a good thing out of the war.

But that was some way into the future. For the present we were enjoying life amongst these colourful neighbours and, for all we knew, we were there for keeps.

Chapter 8

Life on the Three-legged Stool

Once we had our first few cows, life became much more bound by routine. Come what may, cows have to be milked morning and evening and it is no small job, involving as it does, fetching them in for a start, maybe from a distant field, washing their udders and then the milking itself, getting the churns to the road for collection, driving the cows to the fields again and, finally, mucking out the cowshed. All this, except the cowshed cleaning, must be done before breakfast– 'We do a day's work before most people start' is a farming tenet – and then again in the evening. Not that it worried us much at that early stage, with only a handful of milkers, pleasant summer weather and plenty of daylight.

The business of milking a cow was, of course, something I'd never done before. It looks so easy when one sees a skilled hand milker filling the pail almost as if she is opening a tap, with no apparent effort and the frothing milk rising rapidly as you watch. But, in my opinion, it's about as easy as playing a Liszt piano transcription in a storm at sea, with the instrument's lid likely to fall on your fingers at any moment. No one, I'm sure, would deny that it's a knack and one that takes some acquiring. In my case I never appeared to get any better. It seemed to me to call for sheer strength, rather than skill, but this theory is clearly disproved by the ease with which the slightest of dairy maids can do the job, so I just had to accept the galling fact that I was thoroughly incompetent at it and struggle on as best I could.

While I was milking Hyacinth, Bill would do the others, all of them more difficult for one reason or another. One little irritation that even Hyacinth was not above perpetrating is for the cow to shift its weight to and fro from one back leg to the other. This has the unfortunate effect of squashing the milker against the belly of the neighbouring cow and, when the udder is large, of stretching one's arms to the limit. Not a few cows go one better by lifting the nearside leg in an effort to step over the bucket, even bringing the foot down into one's hard-earned spoils. The vicious kicker is also by no means rare, usually due to mishandling in its youth, and this really does call for skill and guts on the part of the milker, for a cow's kick can break a man's arm. Short of strapping the kicker's back legs together, which we resorted to in our time, the cow can often be restrained by lifting one of its front legs off the ground and thus reducing the purchase it can get to permit the kick. This charming little job often fell to my lot, though in all conscience it was preferable to Bill's situation in the firing line. I would first lift the leg in the fashion of a blacksmith and his horse, holding it bent while the cow became more and more agitated about being milked, and subsequently nearly rupture myself in the effort to stop her kneeling down, which she had to do before she could let fly with her back leg.

The second of the good trio amongst the

Captain's handovers was a fine beast with antler-like horns and a haughty demeanour, called Snowdrop. When I dared to stroke her neck at tying-up time, she would dip the nearest antler at me as if to say, 'Watch it, Tosh, and don't take liberties with ladies!' Like Hyacinth, she proved to maintain a high yield rather than give a spectacular amount at the start of each lactation and she, too, contributed many calves to the herd over the years.

The third of the trio, one Mistletoe, an altogether smaller cow, taught me an early lesson in the matter of correct fastening of the cowshed ties. Seeing her standing in her rightful place and enjoying some titbits in the manger below I rashly leant across her head to tie the chain instead of going between the two standings as is the accepted method. Without warning she brought her head up sharply just as I was fully stretched, catching the point of her nearside horn under my chin and giving me a brilliant glimpse of the firmament en passant. Amazingly enough there wasn't even any blood to staunch, and I gave silent thanks to my guardian angel that Mistletoe's horns were blunt-ended, unlike most of the others. Even so, I still come back to earth with a start sometimes when dozing off, at the thought of what might have happened had it been Snowdrop of the antler horns instead of Mistletoe of the blunt ones.

Of the remaining three founder-member cows one, called Lilac, made her presence felt from the start. For one thing she was 'boss cow', which is to say she always led the others, who were afraid of her. I believe there is a boss cow in all herds and a certain amount of fighting takes place to decide the issue, much on the lines of herds of wild animals. In some strange way the mere possession of horns seems to bring out aggressive instincts and this is why most modern herds are dehorned; it saves the farmer no end of trouble from 'hikes' as the horn injuries are called, and helps the milk yields by eliminating fear and promoting contentment, even if it detracts from looks. When Lilac came to us she was 'dry' and, despite being far gone in the family way, she could break out of any field we put her in – straight through the thickest hedge, if necessary. Bill was tickled to find that she would march straight over to the landlord's domain to raid his hay barn, which she knew well, or sample his best field of grass. Not till she'd had time for a good fill would we 'notice' her absence and set off to retrieve her.

Bill was, from the start, extremely careful about washing the utensils thoroughly. The rather officious Mr Morgan from the Ministry had given us a lecture about keeping the walls scrubbed in the cowshed and other points he'd be keeping his eye on, but Bill was sure that cleanliness of utensils was the only thing that really mattered.

'He can't do anything to revoke our licence unless we get some milk returned by the creamery,' said Bill. 'So it's simply a case of being doubly careful about washing and sterilising the buckets and things. The secret is to wash everything thoroughly in cold water first, then a hot wash with detergent and, lastly, to swill in hypochlorite.'

'And what's that corrugated metal thing in the dairy?'

'That's the cooler. Just eyewash, of course!'

'How d'you mean, eyewash? Why don't we use it? It must have cost enough!'

'Oh, yes, it cost thirty quid, but it's a sight easier to stick the churn under the tap as we're doing.'

'Well, why on earth waste thirty pounds?'

'For the simple reason that we had to have one in order to qualify for a milk producer's licence. The point is that the quicker milk is cooled the longer it will keep – and it happens straightaway with those things.'

'Then why not use it?'

'Because it would take time to wash properly, and we've got enough to wash without that thing!' explained Bill patiently.

Having only one churn, and that barely half full in the early stages, it was a simple enough matter to do without the cooler. In hot weather we used the old trick of wrapping it in a sack before putting the tap to dribble on it. It always struck me as crazy that creameries sent out their lorries to collect the milk at the crack of dawn, no doubt with a view to getting the morning's milk to market as soon as possible. In practice it meant starting to milk so early that most farmers got round it by not including the morning's milk, but keeping it for the following day's collection, with the result that the creameries succeeded only in getting staler milk by trying to force the farmers' hands with their early collections.

The only papers we ever saw, apart from the local rag which we got once a week from the shop, were the Sunday ones, delivered about lunch-time by a typically inquisitive village lad who suffered from a cleft palate.

'Whath the little green chimley, then?' he inquired when I went to the door on one of his early visits. He seemed mystified at the information that it was the ventilator of our new Elsan, of which we were rather proud, and which was such an improvement on the outdoor model across the vegetable garden.

'Not much of a day, Glyn,' I said, by way of passing chat. 'Whatever happened to that fine spell we were supposed to be getting?'

'Antie was comin',' he replied in his rich Welsh brogue, 'but she got a puncher! That'll be tenpence for them papers, then.'

'Oh, yes. Just a minute – I think I've left my jacket in the cowshed.'

'Thilly mugger!'

'What was that?' I snapped, suddenly conscious of the fact that hardened N.C.O.'s would have jumped at my lightest word not so long ago and here was this whippersnapper calling me rude names, if I had heard right.

'Thilly mugger!' he repeated, blandly. 'You thould 'ave mrought it with you.'

Bill, who had overheard the conversation while putting the finishing touches to our Sunday lunch, was vastly amused and I reflected ruefully that I could hardly hope for much respect now that I was little more than a farm hand, and on one of the poorest farms for miles around at that. But the expression, complete with Glyn's odd pronunciation, took its place amongst many others we acquired at Vendre as part of our stock-in-trade.

Chapter 9

Cows in the Wood

'I've got to go down to Kropje's after lunch,' announced Bill one morning. 'He wants a hand with his bit of corn. If you'd get the cows in about the usual time, I'll be back for the milking.'

The only difficulty I could envisage was the occasional cow going to the wrong place in the cowshed, but I reckoned I could cope with that easily enough. And, even if I couldn't, it would not be the end of the world.

'O.K. I'll make a start if you're late!' I said cheerfully.

There was nothing very pressing for me to do that afternoon so I set about clearing the kitchen table of the previous week's build-up. It never occurred to us to wash up anything after a meal; we did well if we remembered to put the lid on the jam-pot, wrap the butter against flies and stick the meat in the safe. As a result things tended to build up rapidly and it was often a bit difficult to find a space for the next repast. Every now and again, however, usually on a Sunday morning when there was a joint to be cooked, I would set about the considerable task of (a) clearing the table right down to the cloth, and (b) washing up the stack of dirty crocks and cutlery. This job, combined with the preparation of the lunch, usually took me the entire morning but on this particular afternoon I set about it with a will, for there was something else I wanted to do: I wished to try my hand at baking the fruit cake I'd been given such careful instructions about before leaving home, and was anxious to see what I could do with Bill out of the way.

I duly stirred the mixture to what I considered was the right consistency, lit the two oil burners of our posh new stove and placed the large tin in the oven according to instructions. It was a tricky business adjusting the wicks to burn with the recommended blue flames, but after a good deal of fiddling I got them right. By this time it was getting on towards cow-fetching time so I had a spot of tea, checked my burners once more and sallied forth to enjoy the afternoon sunshine, and show Bill that I could be relied on to carry out a fairly basic farming task, novice though I was.

'Come on, Trigger, old fellow. Let's go and get 'em!' So saying, I unhitched the puppy's chain and set off with him along the lane towards the four-acre field. This was the sort of job I always enjoyed: all the pleasant sights and scents of the summer countryside and the simple enough task of rounding up a few cows. Of course, they will never leave the field of their own volition in summer – the grass is too good – so there's nothing for it but to drive them out. Even this is often frustrated by the boss cow planting herself squarely in the gateway and refusing to let the others pass. Inevitably, this had to happen on this particular day, and all my shouting failed to budge old Lilac. Rather rashly, as I realised afterwards, I flung my heavy stick at her, catching her a telling blow on the tender base of the tail. It certainly did the trick, however, and she started to trot down the lane towards the farm buildings. I hoped Bill wouldn't turn up just then as he was always saying, 'Don't make them run – it upsets their milking to get them excited.'

And to make matters worse, Lilac was very full in milk, having recently calved.

'That'll teach the old devil to block up the gateway!' I chortled, happily, as the others followed more sedately down the lane.

'Come along, now! COW! COW!' I bawled in professional fashion as I brought up the rear into the yard. A pleasant life this farming, I thought, once you begin to know the ropes.

Suddenly I noticed, to my consternation, that instead of turning in through the open cowshed door, as they'd always done in the past, the leading cows were filing straight past and heading up the pathway that led to the woods above. Then I saw the reason: the blighted Lilac, tail in air, no doubt because of my ungentlemanly treatment of her in the gateway, was a hundred yards out in front and going well.

'Jeepers! I must head her off before she's loose in that wood, Trigger, or we'll never get her back!' I gasped, dashing across the yard and cutting straight up through a near-vertical field, to scramble through the top hedge just in time to cut off the chase and turn them all back down the track again towards the farm. Badly blown as I was, after my uphill sprint, I offered a silent prayer that they would go in this time, now that Lilac was no longer in the lead. But not a bit of it! Straight past the open door they strode, all a bit excited by this time, and out into the lane once more.

'Blast and confound the bastards! What the hell's got into them?' I cried, and found myself sprinting once more across country to head them off. Perspiring freely, I succeeded in turning the brutes round once again and started to take them as slowly as possible for yet another try, talking soothingly in the hope of calming them a bit: 'THERE's good girls... NOTHING to worry about... COME along then...'

Lilac was in front again, but walking now. Would she go in this time or wouldn't she? She seemed normal enough... She stopped opposite the door... She hesitated, and I held my breath... Go on, you old fool! But all my willing came to naught. She moved off up the track again, the others in line behind. It was the last straw.

'YOU BLOODY OLD SOD!' I yelled, sprinting after Lilac's receding form in a vain attempt to get within range for a repetition of the stick-throwing treatment I'd applied so successfully in the gateway earlier.

If the cows hadn't been excited before,

they certainly were now! Tails up, they were dashing at a fast canter up into the woods. I had completely shot my bolt in my vain effort to get even with Lilac and could only look on forlornly at my receding charges. The prospect of repeating the performance ad infinitum was more than I could take, exhausted as I now was.

'WHAT ON EARTH'S GOING ON?' came Bill's voice from the yard below, and I turned to see him staring in horror at his precious cows frisking in the wood above.

'These —— cows won't go into the cowshed!' I croaked. 'They've walked past it about fifty times and now they've gone berserk!'

'I can see that! What's got them so worked up?'

'God knows,' I hedged. 'They're barmy, if you ask me!'

No doubt Bill could see that I was as distraught as the cows, and he didn't probe further. Between us we eventually retrieved our precious animals from the wood and got them tied up in their places without further trouble. Bill looked a bit pensive while all this was going on but, as usual when I behaved in an un-farmer-like fashion, he refrained from saying so.

'Anyway,' I said, rather shamefacedly, 'I've got a nice surprise for you to make up for things – I baked a cake this afternoon… Oh, Lord! Excuse me, I've just remembered something!'

As I dashed across to the house I noticed black smoke coming from the partly-opened kitchen window. The stove! Rushing into the kitchen, I was pulled up short by utter blackness – not a glimmer of light in any direction and the sun was still shining outside! I felt my way across to where the oil stove was sited at the other side of the room, inhaling the most evil paraffin odours, to find the two burners pouring forth thick black fumes from yellow flames a foot high. Trying to hold my breath, I hastily turned down the wicks to zero, flung open the windows as far as possible and swam out again to the fresh air, catching in festoons of black stuff hanging from the beams as I did so. Our beautiful kitchen was filthier than I could ever have imagined possible and it took us days to clean up the mess.

'The cake will be ruined,' laughed Bill, when he'd taken in the full extent of the 'nice surprise' I'd promised. 'You'd better leave it to me next time!'

I'd quite forgotten the cake in the excitement but, sure enough, it was a write-off. Even Elsie and Gertie turned up their noses at it.

Chapter 10

A Wild-duck Chase

The season of mists and mellow fruitfulness – or more significantly, of frosts and the drawing in of nights – was upon us. Our woods took on their glorious hues and we fell to lighting the kitchen fire quite often. No longer could we do our pre-breakfast jobs in daylight, and the evening milking gradually slipped later to permit the full use of daylight for other work besides routine.

With the passing of the equinox life certainly lost some of its initial magic. Of course we had no electricity, the only house boasting it for miles around being the Captain's, and that provided by his own plant. The oil pressure lamp became our standby, both in the house and outside, and when its constant hiss got on our nerves we switched to a stately Aladdin, complete with tall glass chimney but too cumbersome to take outdoors.

In early autumn, before the weather really broke, we spent a lot of time in the woods, felling small oaks for fencing stakes and building our stock of firewood. There can be few more pleasant tasks, in the hazy autumn sunshine, than wielding an axe to good effect among the russet trees. Bill was something of an artist with the axe and could cut a perfect stake in half the strokes it took me, the brushwood neatly stacked and the stake-end sharply pointed. With the ground still hard we were able to take the Old Girl up the track and fill her with logs and stakes as often as we needed. Elsie and Gertie, too, enjoyed the autumn woodlands, rooting about for acorns to their hearts' delight. We even built them a shack in the woods, with a sizeable run made of pig netting to keep them in, but not before we'd lost them once or twice. More than once we took up their evening feed to find them gone, but we only had to bang their buckets loudly enough for them to reappear at the double.

As the dry, crisp days of September and October gave way to the rain and mud of November, Vendre Fach took another step away from the delightful little farmstead with which we had started. We began to see what sixty inches of rain a year means in practice and I can still see, in my mind's eye, the 'sheets' of rain apparently suspended across the steep little valley for weeks at a stretch. No more pleasant daydreams while rounding up the cows, or leaning on a gate to pass the time of day, for now the fields were quagmires, especially round the gates. Even cows detest the driving rain, and huddle round the gateways long before the normal time for coming in. We shared a mud and water world, plus the endless job of drying out our clothes.

In this transformed environment we found time to think of other things besides the work, for a change. I managed to find a battery wireless set on one of my trips to town, to augment the wind-up gramophone that had provided our only music up till then. We even succeeded in finding a local woman to come in and 'do' for us once a week. The kitchen table reappeared twice weekly, in consequence, instead of just on Sundays as before.

Maida Granitt, as we christened our tough little Welsh help, did a lot for our faltering morale with her weekly visit, for not only did she bring a badly needed touch of the duster and polish to our little house, but she regularly cooked us a substantial dish or two to see us through till the following Sunday. We really did appreciate Maida's efforts, and on the rare occasions when something prevented her coming we were dashed indeed.

Every now and again, usually when rain was preventing any useful work outdoors, we would sit down to what we came to know as 'a financial'. Quite early on we worked out, I remember, that our total outgoings on the domestic front amounted to around £450 a year. Looking back on that figure, it seems a small cost to pay for running a household but, at the time, we were rather shocked to realise that we had to make that much profit before we could so much as break even. I often think that when people expect higher wages as some sort of divine right, they should stop to consider how hard it is to make even a basic living when working for oneself. At one of these sessions we decided to get some more cows before winter set in, rather than in the spring as had been our intention in view of the limited quantity of hay we'd inherited from the Captain.

'It boils down to the fact that we're living almost entirely on what goes into the daily milk churn,' said Bill, through the pipe smoke, 'and, even with the premiums, it's only half a crown a gallon. If we don't expand our herd till spring comes, we'll soon be living off capital.'

'And what about the hay problem?'

'Well, we won't have to feed much before Christmas the way the grass is holding out, and no doubt the old man will sell us a few tons if we run short.'

We also decided at about this time to keep the two litters of piglets on till they reached bacon weight, rather than sell them as weaners at about eight weeks old.

'There's good money in fattening at the moment,' explained Bill, 'but plenty of work involved, of course. We might build up a second enterprise by buying in weaners later on, over and above Elsie's and Gertie's litters, if all goes well.'

'Our only other income is the eggs, I suppose?'

'Yes, and it's hardly worth the effort of washing the things, but every little helps, of course.'

And so it came about that our 'herd' grew by fifty per cent, with three more milkers, towards the end of the year. Unfortunately, there were no farm sales just then, so Bill was obliged to try his luck at the mart, a risky thing to do as nobody sells a cow in the market without good reason. In the event we were fairly lucky with what we got although, as we feared, they all proved to have some hidden snag to account for their being up for sale.

The star was a really magnificent cow called Jane, in a class above anything else we had, who was giving no less than seven gallons a day when she arrived with a fine heifer calf. Her snag, as we were to find to our cost, was that she was exceptionally hard and slow to milk.

The second cow was a prettily marked and very friendly two-year old called Minnie, which Bill had bought quite cheaply, to compensate for the eighty guineas he'd had to pay for Jane. Minnie was to prove a delightful cow in all respects save one: she objected strongly to being milked, and was a 'kicker' from the start.

The last of the trio was a timid little Jersey cross which Bill christened Denise for no better reason than that she had an odd way of going down on 'de knees' when eating hay.

'But why the mixture?' I asked Bill on his return from his exciting day at the market. 'I thought we were supposed to be building up a famous herd of Ayrshires?'

'I reckon she should help to push up the butterfat content of the milk, which is a bit borderline at the moment, and we can always weed her out later on if we want to,' he explained.

So we now had a mealy-muzzled Jersey to give variety to the herd, and we'd got away from the Captain's flower names. Counting the three calves – Jane's little beauty of which we expected great things, Lilac's born in September, and the third from one of the Captain's also-rans – we could boast a round dozen head of cattle by the time Christmas came round. We christened all the calves after members of our own family, a compliment not always appreciated when we were honoured by visits from our nearest and dearest in the course of time.

'What are we going to do about Christmas dinner?' I inquired one evening as the great day approached. 'It's hardly worth getting a turkey just for the two of us, is it? And chicken seems a bit feeble.'

'I wish I could bag one of those wild duck that come into the bottom meadow every night,' returned Bill. 'I heard them coming in about half an hour ago, but it was much too dark for a shot.'

'Well, we've got that big lantern torch of yours?' I hazarded, knowing nothing about shooting.

'Hmm! I wonder,' said Bill with a whistle. 'I might get a shot if you wield the torch for me. Come on, let's have a go!'

The night was as black as any I ever knew as we set off down the steep field that led towards the river, and started to feel our way through the copse bordering the meadow. 'Wild goose' rather than 'duck' was the sort of chase that came to mind as we crept stealthily through the copse, trying to avoid the double hazard of twigs in the eye and underfoot.

'They're usually in the far corner where the river's deeper,' whispered Bill. 'We'll creep as near as we can and, the moment they get up, aim the torch into their midst.'

I've done some daft things in my life, I thought, as we moved one step at a time across the frozen meadow, and a strong feeling came over me that there were no birds there anyway. I was also a shade apprehensive of having my head blown off in the dark.

All was 'deathly 'ush', to use one of Watkyn's favourite expressions, when suddenly, straight ahead of us, came a whirring of wings. I flicked down the switch and aimed at the noises off, nothing whatever being visible to my straining eyes ... both barrels of the twelve-bore blasted off unpleasantly close to my left ear, and we were dashing forward through the frosty grass... 'You've hit one! Fantastic!' I yelled excitedly as we came up to a flapping bird and grabbed it.

'Where's the other?' puffed Bill. 'I'm sure I got a second one – listen!' And, sure enough, we heard scuffling beyond the hedge, which turned out to be another beauty.

'Well, knock me down with a feather!' I gurgled, astounded. 'I didn't think there was a hope in hell! How on earth could you see what you were shooting at? I couldn't see anything but the beam!'

'D'you mean to say you didn't pick out that second one deliberately? You held it in the beam like a searchlight with a bomber!'

'Well, I'm blessed,' I said. 'I honestly didn't see a thing!'

So we didn't do so badly for Christmas after all. Wild duck, we told ourselves, is a cut above common turkey and, after Bill had given his gourmet's touch to the dressing of the birds and all the trimmings, it proved a memorable meal. Kind relations had sent us mince pies and a bottle of hock and we did ourselves proud despite our self-inflicted banishment from family and friends.

Chapter 11

Winter Sports

As the New Year brought its increasingly hard weather, our routine jobs on the farm increased steadily to match, particularly in the matter of the score or so of pigs we were fattening as baconers. Each week that passed saw a substantial increase in the quantity of gruel recommended by the experts for producing the best bacon and, this being our first sally into the pig-fattening business, we struck religiously to the book. Goodness knows how many buckets of the heavy swill had to be mixed and carried up the steep yard to the fattening quarters twice a day.

'The best of them should be ready at six months,' explained Bill when they were beginning to approach the right size. 'The problem is to get the weights right, though, as obviously they must all go together and be within the limits laid down if they're to qualify for the top grade.'

'How are pigs usually weighed, then?'

'A pig-weighing machine is a sort of cage built on a sensitive platform, rather like a small-scale weighbridge.'

'Well, how about making a cage and suspending it on that strong balance you picked up at that auction sale in November?' I suggested.

And so we set about constructing a Heath Robinson device for weighing the live bacon, which we came to know as the 'Shortback-and-sides' on account of its proving a fearful squash for the longer pigs in any group. It was a masterpiece of metal bars and struts, held with nails and wire on to a stout wooden base and complete with doors at either end as entry and exit. We rigged it up in one of the outbuildings, with the heavy balance hooked securely to a large beam and linked with chains to an outsize lever which had started life as the elevating handle of a horse-drawn hayrake.

The very first time we used our great invention, however, disaster struck, for no sooner had we whisked the first customer off the ground and locked the lever in the down position so that the cage swung freely at about waist height for weighing purposes than he fought his way out of the side, and in doing so tore a five-inch gash in his belly, as well as doing serious damage to the masterpiece.

'Blast it all!' cursed Bill. 'I thought it was solid enough to hold an ox! These nails aren't strong enough – we'll have to get Watkyn to weld it.'

'Look at the gash in his stomach!' I exclaimed, eyeing the unfortunate baconer which was cowering against the wall and returning the compliment with interest.

'Serves him right, he's wrecked the thing. Would you credit it?'

'Well, we've seen enough to know they're a long way off bacon weight,' I said. 'That chap is one of the biggest and he's only about seven stone.'

The cage was duly taken up in the Old Girl to be welded and, thereafter, proved a boon. After a little experience we devised a crafty technique for getting the pigs into it without having to resort to the physical persuasion tactics called for at the start. The secret was to build a little tunnel out of straw bales for them to enter by.

A few days after the accident to the cage, however, Bill came down from the morning pig feed with a worried expression.

'Young Percy, the one that gashed himself, has gone off his food,' he confided. 'That means the vet and quick, or we'll lose him. I'll 'phone Lewis from the village on my way to Caersws, but I'm afraid you'll have to see him as I shan't be back till late this afternoon. He'll probably just inject the pig or something of the sort, so you needn't worry,' he added, noticing my look of consternation at the prospect. I never did relish the vet's visits, for he had a nasty way of getting one to hold the animal while he performed some barbaric treatment.

'Well, let's hope you're right!' I mumbled, a bit apprehensively.

Gwyn Lewis, the young vet from Llanfair, like many of the people of those parts, didn't waste time on pleasantries. But for all that we soon formed a very high opinion of his ability.

'Hot water, soap and towel,' he snapped in reply to my attempt at a greeting. We soon learnt that this was his invariable order, whether he needed the items or not. In this instance he only used them to wash himself afterwards, I remember.

'Right, hold him down!' he commanded when we'd dragged the hundred-pound baconer out on to the yard by the ears. Frightful squeals ensued as I struggled to throw the ailing pig on its side and hold it there with my knee in its shoulder.

Kneeling alongside, Lewis contrived to empty out a handful of white sulphanilamide powder and, without any preliminary cleansing of the wound, started kneading the powder into it with both hands, chatting casually about the weather as he did so. After several minutes of this treatment, which must have been pretty agonising for the patient, the gash was stuffed solid with powder.

'Right, leave 'im go!' ordered Lewis, getting to his feet.

'Do we have to bathe it, or anything?' I inquired, tentatively.

'Naw, mun. 'E'll be all right! I'll have a wash and be on my way.'

And so it proved. Percy was back on his grub next morning and was one of the best when he finally went for the chop a few weeks later.

Although it was a great help to know the weights accurately, we were rather shattered to find they were nowhere near bacon weight by the time six months were up.

'It must be this confounded hard weather that's slowing things down,' sighed Bill after a disappointing session with the Shortback-and-sides. 'Too much food-energy is being used up in keeping them warm.'

I could see the point. Soon after Christmas the weather had turned extremely cold, so much so that Bill and I had given up undressing at night, preferring to go to bed fully clothed. The poor pigs, by contrast, had just a bit of straw to insulate them from the concrete floor, and their only ploy was to sleep in a heap, which was no doubt quite effective but evidently not the complete answer to their problem.

'Of course, the big breeders have electric heating in the fattening pens nowadays,' explained Bill, 'and low insulated roofs to contain the warmth. We can't do anything like that, so we'll just have to keep them a few weeks extra till they made the grade. It's sickening, of course, with food at such a price, but it should work the other way in the summer.'

And so we battled on, with the occasional weighing session to bolster our morale. Struggling up the steep yard with a full bucket of gruel in each hand had been heavy work before the place became icebound; now it was positively killing, especially in rubber boots which afford no grip. But at long last the scale registered what we'd been waiting for, the pigs were duly entered with the Ministry and a haulier booked to collect them. This was a big moment for us, not only because we were anxious to be rid of our heavy feeding operation, but also because the sale represented a major cash item by this time, with foodstuff bills mounting alarmingly.

When the appointed morning for collection came round Bill and I were up earlier than usual and pleasantly excited at the prospect of getting the pigs safely off. The lorry was due about breakfast time and we wanted to get the milking out of the way before it came.

'He's going to have a job backing up the yard with all this ice about,' remarked Bill while we were still milking. 'Even the muck heap is like a rock this morning – I couldn't shift that fork you left in it.'

The approaching daylight was just beginning to reveal the full extent of the glittering frost when Trigger's sharp ears detected the approach of the lorry. A few moments later and his barking was drowned by the heavy engine as the vehicle swung along the bottom of the yard with its lights ablaze.

Ifor Pritchard was an extremely well-fed

young bull of a fellow whose father was a successful farmer on the better land beyond Llanfair. They had done very well during the war and had branched out as contractors and hauliers. Ifor, the son, was the chief operator on this side of the business, and it was he who now swung his huge lorry across our yard. After pushing its nose right up against the tall hedge near the cowshed, he proceeded to take a 'run' in reverse. The tyres spun till they smoked with burning rubber despite the ice, but Ifor, showing an admirable disregard for the damage, made two or three more runs to get as near the pens as the conditions would allow. Heaving on the brake with a gargantuan tug and hopping athletically down from the cab with a curt 'Best I can do!' to Bill and me, he revealed himself to be very poshly attired in a loud 'bookie suit', all ready for a big day at the market.

'We'll 'ave to manhandle 'em to the bottom of the ramp,' he announced, pulling down the great back door of the lorry which, with its side 'gates', formed the ramp that the animals would mount by. 'One at a time is best,' he added, rather to the surprise of Bill and myself who had hoped to be able to drive them up en masse with the aid of two rolls of pig netting we had put ready. However, we were happy to bow to Ifor's long experience, especially as he plunged, without further discussion, into the nearest pig-pen.

A moment later Ifor emerged, wrestling in very professional fashion with a pig which he held by one ear and its tail.

'Naw! I'll manage 'im!' he shot at Bill as, with sundry oaths, Ifor propelled his unwilling charge towards the foot of the ramp. Whether it was the steepness of the slope, or the ice, or a combination of factors, that upset Ifor's long-practised skill in pig-handling, Bill and I could not be sure but, whatever the underlying cause, the baconer somehow succeeded in wresting its ear free of his grip and, in darting back through his legs, completely upended fat Ifor, throwing him flat on his back, posh suit and all.

'BLOODY GOOD START!!' yelled Ifor with immense power and feeling, as he struggled to his feet. Fortunately for us, the errant pig had run into an open pen nearby but, frost or no, Ifor's suit had picked up a fair plastering of Vendre Fach's principal by-product. Bill and I dared not look at one another for a moment, but plunged hastily into the pen to grab a pig each and hide our grins.

I found the two-eared technique infinitely

preferable to Ifor's ear-and-tail system. Even so, it involved more than one ride for me on the animals' backs in my desperate effort to hold on. We all knew that if one pig escaped we could be held up for hours. The worst that happened to me was to lose my cap during one rodeo interlude, but I retrieved it undamaged in time for the next ride.

At last all twenty baconers were safely aboard, the gates closed on them, the ramp lifted and Ifor was swinging the big lorry out of the yard.

'That should teach him not to dress up like the dog's dinner when he comes here!' laughed Bill, and somehow Ifor's heartfelt cry of 'Bloody good start!' joined certain other apt phrases we met along the way, and became a part of our farm vocabulary from that day on.

That first winter proved far and away the coldest of the three we were to experience at Vendre Fach. It was one of those years when the weather forecasts keep promising a thaw 'next week', but something always happens to postpone its arrival. Although life was harder in many respects, however, it was not without its compensations. Perhaps top of the list was the fact that we could do without the wretched gumboots that a farmer tends to live in at most seasons. We could even pop out of doors in our slippers, an action normally quite out of the question. Worries about cooling the milk certainly vanished and the business of being squashed between two heaving cows, even the effort of milking, became quite pleasurable for a change, thanks to the warmth being generated.

We had long realised that the kitchen fire did little or nothing to warm the room, especially in windy weather when a powerful current of air was sucked up the huge chimney. Sitting in front of a good old blaze was a frustrating experience as one's face would burn while a perishing wind behind shrivelled up one's neck and ears. We even tried erecting a barrier of curtains one Sunday, in an effort to snatch an hour or two's comfort, but the draught was so strong that, even with the curtains wrapped round the backs of our chairs, the wind still managed to blow in underneath to make the place untenable.

For the most part we relied for warmth on one of those old, black, cylindrical paraffin heaters with holes in the top and a little shutter to let the heat out. This we left on all day and used as a hand-warmer in the limited time we spent indoors. Upstairs was like an icebox, though, which prompted Bill to pull the postman's leg one morning.

'And how are you boys managing in this hard weather?' asked the kindly old fellow who had worries of his own to cope with on the icy roads.

'None too badly, thanks,' returned Bill. 'Apart from the jerry freezing up and the ink, of course. We haven't been able to write a letter for weeks.'

'Oh, dear me, indeed. I'm very sorry about that,' was the solemn-faced reply, and it was a bit embarrassing to get condolences from near strangers, sometimes months afterwards, of what they'd heard had befallen the 'bedroom furniture' at Vendre, as they put it in sepulchral tones. It slowly sank in on us that one had to be careful about flippant jokes in deepest Wales.

One thing that did freeze up, though, much to our consternation, was the old car. We religiously drained her every evening by means of small taps at the bottom of the engine, the expense of using anti-freeze never even entering our heads. Needing her again first thing in the morning to take the milk churn up the lane, we would simply fill her with hot water, give two or three turns of the handle, and away she went every time.

But one night the inevitable happened: we forgot to drain her, and on going to start her in the morning I was aghast to see what looked like small exhaust pipes curving downwards on both sides of the engine. They proved to be of solid ice protruding from small apertures in the side of the cylinder block, rather in the way that frozen milk will sometimes lift off the bottle cap and protrude upwards. We were certain we had wrecked our pride and joy and sent an SOS to Watkyn to come as soon as possible.

'Well, you boys was lucky, that's all I can say!' declared Watkyns when he arrived later in the day. 'Them icicles by there have forced out the little "pennies" built into the side of the block to save it breaking. She'll be all right once the thaw comes, I shouldn't wonder. We'll just have to put back them little discs.'

And so it proved. The old car was none the worse for her ordeal, though we had to take up the milk churn by wheelbarrow until she thawed out.

'Marvellous Old Girl!' we said in unison.

Chapter 12

Wheelbarrow Power

Perhaps the key date of the whole farming calendar is March 25th, generally known as 'Lady Day'. This is the date when rents are due and farms normally change hands if they're going to do so. It divides off, better than any other moment, the end of one farming year from the start of the next, for by the time Lady Day comes along the whole cycle has run its course, the fodder from the previous harvest is about exhausted, and the farmer's world stands poised to begin the whole process over again.

One major task remained for us still to do before Lady Day, after the thaw arrived in early March. The farmyard manure, known politely as FYM, but more generally as plain 'muck', had still to be taken to the fields.

'Getting the muck out' is one of the milestones of the farmer's year, involving, as it does, the thorough cleansing of all calf pens in addition to the removal of the midden.

Calves, delightful creatures that they are, have to be rather pampered with straw and good dry conditions if they are to do well. Surprisingly enough, it is wiser to keep them in their smelly pens until they are at least six months old, rather than let them out into the fields where they tend to pick up 'husk' and other ailments from the grass infected by adult cows. The job of mucking out calf pens, which can contain the compressed remains of a whole year's bedding, is not one to be sneezed at. Thanks to the depth of the 'carpet', the calf is often half-way to the roof of its shed after all this time, so the unfortunate 'mucker-out' has extremely cramped space in which to wield his fork, quite apart from the heaviness of the work occasioned by its having been so compacted. The last straw, so to speak, is the powerful ammonia stench which does little to help in the heavy breathing that the work brings on.

Nowadays, I believe, this job is done easily enough by machines but not so at Vendre Fach in my day. Real farmers, even in those days, did, however, boast machines called 'muck-spreaders', ingenious cart-like metal trucks which both carry the manure to the field and spread it around by means of spinning spikes. At Vendre we had only the wheelbarrow for both parts of the operation.

'How many fields do you reckon to do with this lot, then?' I queried between gasps. 'I should think there's enough here to do the whole farm!'

'There isn't, you know,' returned Bill, shifting about twice the work I was doing, as usual. 'It doesn't go very far, this stuff, especially when spread by hand, as we're going to have to do.'

'Spread by hand, did you say?' I said weakly.

'Well, by fork I mean, really,' laughed Bill. 'The drill is to cover the field with little mounds and then to fling it around with forks afterwards.'

'Hmm! I see. Sounds like a nice little job at that.'

'It's this barrow business of taking it out that's going to take the time,' Bill went on. 'Not that it's very far, and it's all downhill, so it could be worse. I'm thinking of the field on the left, below the lane; that's where the kale and spuds are going, and some roots at the bottom, I expect.'

We started with the muck from the calf pens; across the yard, along the lane, fortunately slightly downhill in the section nearest the house, and through the gate about fifty yards away on the left. Once in the field life became a lot more tricky, the long frost having left very little grip underfoot and a great deal of effort being called for, in consequence, to keep one's balance with the heavy barrow. To begin with, though, the haul through the field was comparatively short as we tipped our loads, three to a mound, along the lane-side hedge. The return to base with empty barrow was also comparatively simple, unlike the slithering struggle it became as we progressed further down the steep field.

When we came to start on the huge job of moving the midden, I reflected that I had personally built almost the entire edifice myself, one barrow-load at a time, since the job of doing the cowshed had become rather exclusively mine. It was a task I always enjoyed, strangely enough, especially the washing down at the end, with the satisfying swish of the heavy broom on the cross-grooved concrete floors.

'So your plaything will soon be no more,' joked Bill as we prepared to remove the mountain with our teaspoons.

'I'll be sad to see it go,' I sighed. 'It's quite a monument to my labours, really, isn't it?'

'I know one thing,' said Bill. 'Next year's

model won't be a solid affair like this one. Not if we go ahead with that whey-feeding idea for the pigs, I was telling you about – it'll be all over the yard *and* in the house if we're not careful! Dreadful stuff whey, they tell me.'

'Oh, Lord! Yes, I see what you mean. Not a pleasant prospect.'

We must have spent about a fortnight on that charming little farm chore. Loading the barrow was, of course, child's play, but slithering and tacking down the precipitous field with one's arms starting from their sockets, became progressively more wearing. The lower parts of the field, away from the top hedges were like a skating rink, trebling the effort required to keep one's balance with the heaped barrow. There was no option but to wear rubber boots, of course, and the dragging back uphill was almost as difficult as the outward journey.

'If this job doesn't kill me, nothing will!' I groaned to Bill in the final stages.

'Cheer up, mun. We should have a trailer by next year, so that should take most of the fun out of it. We'll be able to spread it straight off the trailer, too, which will shorten the job a bit.'

'And when are we going to spread this lot?'

'Next week, I hope. But Gareth has promised to give us a hand. If we all three pitch in we could do it in a day.'

I wasn't exactly looking forward to the spreading but felt it could hardly match the dumping job to which our nice clean yard now bore witness. True to his word, the well-muscled Gareth turned up after breakfast on the Monday, complete with muckfork. Equally important was the fact that he had his powerful wife in tow.

'Eirwen says she'd like to give you boys a lesson in muck-slinging,' explained Gareth, amidst raucous laughter from his spouse. 'It's her favourite job, next to humping slag, isn't it, dear?'

We started, in line, working downfield from the top. By virtue of the varying texture of the commodity concerned, the business of achieving an even spread is extraordinarily tricky, large dollops tending to fly off the fork instead of small ones. The technique is to apply sufficient power to each swing to break up the forkful as it is splattered around. Too often I would find myself having to shake out lumps which had failed to disintegrate, to the detriment of my rate of progress. Before long I was lagging rather sadly behind the other three, but this proved to be not altogether a bad thing when Eirwen's rustic humour started to get the better of her. More than once she deliberately miscued in the direction of both Gareth and Bill, splattering them with muck and provoking gales of laughter on her part.

'Now, give over, you filthy bastard!' shouted Gareth after one playful throw had sprayed his face and clothes.

'Me filthy!' shrieked Eirwen, beside herself with mirth, 'you should look in a mirror, and you'd soon see who's filthy!'

Eirwen's laugh must have been audible for miles around that day, but the job got done in double-quick time, thanks to our two stalwart helpers. Bill, who had been in the line of fire, didn't seem quite to share my view, however, of the value of country humour when working in the fields.

Chapter 13

First Cultivations

The Captain, very decently, offered to have his tractor-man, Charlie, plough the steep field below the house for us where Bill planned to carry out our first cultivations. March winds had dried out the land surprisingly well after the excessively slippery conditions following on from the long freeze, and I was looking forward to getting to grips with the land itself as a change from the animal-tending which had occupied so much of our time since we started.

The day the Captain came over to arrange the details of the ploughing, Bill was busy putting slag on another of our few cultivable fields by hand. This stuff, slag, is a by-product of the iron-smelting industry, rich in phosphorous and consequently a valuable provider of nutrients for the soil. The trouble is that it's a very dark grey, almost black, soot-like substance, much given to blowing around in the slightest breeze, and impossible to apply by hand without getting oneself plastered from head to foot. Now it so happened that Bill used sometimes to go as much as a whole week without shaving, such a time-consuming occupation being considered by him very much in the category of none-productive work. As a result, and by virtue of his exceptionally strong growth of beard, he tended to look quite a ruffian more often than not, and how much more so after an hour or two's walking the fields casting great handfuls of slag around him from a bucket at his chest.

Spotting the Captain's approach down the lane, and unaware of how much slag had become attached to his features, Bill emerged from a gap in the hedge just as the unsuspecting Captain was passing by. Exactly what passed through the military mind at this sudden apparition on a lovely spring morning, it is difficult to say but, according to Bill's account, the Captain's reflexes shot him about two feet into the air which, combining with a strangled gasp of 'Oh, my God!', brought home to Bill the realisation that perhaps he was looking less than his best.

'Just applying a spot of slag, Captain,' he explained, through caked lips. 'Dusty stuff, isn't it?'

'Eh? Oh, I see,' returned the Captain, recovering his composure with an effort. 'Didn't recognise you for a moment, I must say. I thought my sins had caught up with me or something.'

They walked together to the field gate, a little further down the lane.

'Yes, it could probably do with some slag,' observed our landlord, 'but it's a marvellous field, this one, you know. The best on the entire estate, I shouldn't be surprised. It's gone on producing first-rate crops year after year. I wish I'd been able to hang on to it, really, but there w'are, there w'are!'

Bill was surprised at this praise, for, despite its being one of our few fairly level fields, the opinion of the locals about its prowess didn't tally at all. Very much the contrary, in fact. Only the week before, Evans-the-Road had given his considered judgement on it during a break for conversation: 'That field,' he had said with conviction, 'is the worst bit of land any crow ever chose for its droppings!' Indeed, it was partly on the strength of Evans's report that Bill had decided to apply the slag in the first place.

We were slowly beginning to get the measure of the Captain. What at first we had taken for military bluff, and later for lack of farming knowledge, we finally came to recognise as the odd sense of humour it undoubtedly was.

In due course, Charlie, the tractor-man, came to plough the steep field with the Captain's fine David Brown tractor. Despite the dangerous slope, he managed it in a couple of hours and harrowed it afterwards to get a sufficient tilth for our seed and potato sowing. Bill had hired a small hand-trundling machine from the County Agricultural Committee, a thing that looked a bit like a machine used for marking tennis courts and sports fields. With this we could sow one row of seeds at a time, the top half of the field going down mainly to kale and a small piece at the bottom, where it was much less steep, to swedes and mangolds. The space between was eventually planted with seed potatoes with the aid of Gareth's horse and an old-fashioned plough-like implement he had which ridged up the ground for planting and, subsequently buried them by being directed between the planted rows.

I found all this both fascinating and eminently satisfying. To be actually cultivating the ground was not only pleasant in itself, with the dry earth and fine spring weather playing their parts, but it was a much needed change of occupation from the surfeit of animal-tending which made up so much of our lives.

'So what's the next thing this field's going to need?' I asked Bill as we surveyed our week's work in a contented frame of mind.

'Well, the kale and the roots will have to be singled some time next month, of course. That's something to look forward to!'

'I thought kale was just grazed in situ, so to speak?'

'It can be, but you get much more bulk by letting it grow into large leafy plants like cabbages, which means singling to give them room to grow. Marvellous stuff for milk, and cows love it.'

'When d'you reckon to feed it, then?'

'Ideally it's fed in the depths of winter, when there's no fresh grass. Kale can withstand a bit of frost, so it can stay in the ground till it's needed, and there aren't many crops you can do that with,' returned Bill. 'It should be quite a crop with all the muck it's had!'

'I'm dying to see how it all comes up,' I said. 'We'll show Evans-the-Road a thing or two yet.'

Chapter 14

Haymaking by Hand

Spring comes late on the Welsh uplands. There is precious little stirring by the first of April, the traditional start of the grazing season in England. But the grass eventually breaks through and, with the first days of early summer, all thoughts turn to the vital matter of the hay harvest.

There is a magic quality about this time of year, of course. The unaccustomed warmth of the sunshine, the buzzing of the bees and the way in which Nature seems to have suddenly decided to do all she can to help for a change, convince even the most sceptical of her good intentions. The fact that in about one year in five all this promise comes to nothing in the treacherous climate does not enter into the farmer's considerations. He is quite sure this year is going to be a good one as his inborn optimism responds once more to May's warm blandishments. But though it is rare for all crops to be harvested undamaged, even in a 'good year', the therapeutic effect on the farmer of experiencing this delightful season of the year plays a big part in enabling him to cope with the trials and hardships which are his lot. This is the time when the countryside is the place to be and the farmer is not only there but actually working it. For a short spell, at least, he is a hundred per cent happy in what he is doing, and feels in his bones that his is the best of all worlds.

I suppose out of all the haymaking I took part in, at Vendre and elsewhere, that first summer's harvesting has remained most vividly in my memory. And the reason is not hard to find, for not only was it my first experience of this all-important aspect of farming life but it was the only year in which we did the 'making' without any implements whatsoever beyond our hay-forks. If we were not quite back to the days of Evans-the-Road's youthful memories – Kropje lent us his ancient mower to cut all the grass – we were certainly not much advanced. The old taxi came into its own as hay-cart extra-ordinary and we sometimes had the help of our neighbours with the actual hauling but the great bulk of the work was effected by our two-pronged forks, or 'pikes' as they are generally known. And, as with so many basic tasks that came our way in those days, I found myself delighted to be doing it in the primitive fashion, despite the effort and sweat entailed.

As so often happens after a hard winter, the summer proved to be an exceptionally good one, something to do with a continuation of the anticyclonic conditions, I believe. June is the great month for hay-making, of course. May hay being generally considered a bit premature, even in England, while by July the grass is getting rather coarse. In our case, in that first summer at Vendre, we had some heavy crops by early June and, with a rare heatwave upon us and the forecast full of promise, Bill decided to make a start on the sloping meadow above the house.

Old Kropje duly arrived soon after breakfast with his funny little three-wheeled tractor and off Bill went round the undulating edge of the hay-field with Kropje and I following behind to deal with brambles and similar hazards. These old 'horse mowers', easily adapted for towing by a tractor, were much in use at that time amongst the farmers of those parts, though the more affluent brethren on the better land had by then switched to the power-operated type controlled by a touch on the lever of the tractor. But the trailer-mower made an excellent job for about a tenth of the outlay, and I was always fascinated to watch it felling a great swathe of grass as its five-foot blade rattled along, like some sharp-edged snake hidden in the heavy crop. Of course, it jams from time to time and the 'knife' has to be replaced when it starts to lose its edge, but in three or four hours the whole fine field is lying in neat rows and rapidly wilting in the sun. Kropje usually left us to it once we'd completed the outer circuit, and I spent the time walking behind to clear the knife when it jammed, a pretty dicey undertaking I always felt, and one likely to remove a finger at the slightest lapse in concentration.

In ideal weather, as it was for that first field, two or three days in addition to the day of cutting are all that's needed before the hay must be 'turned', each swath methodically forked over so that the underlying grass can gets its turn to wilt in the sun. Our fields at Vendre averaged about four acres in extent and it would take Bill and me a full day to go through it all, turning up the yellowing grass, shaking out a thick patch here and casting aside a thistle there. I always feel that no one really knows the meaning of the word 'work' till he's tried tackling a whole field, be it singling rows of roots, weeding a crop, 'turning' by hand as in the present instance, or any of the other tasks that the farmer faces on a field scale. Certainly it's an invaluable experience in its effect of making all subsequent gardening jobs, and the like, seem child's play by comparison, for to dig over one's kitchen garden or weed a few flower beds can never seem daunting again. But, as if the hard work involved in the various processes of haymaking is not enough, the pleasure of the job is further eroded by the excessive heat of the open field and the exasperating flies, to the point where it often becomes a trial of endurance.

Usually when we were on our own, Bill and I would 'throw down', as the Welsh phrase goes, everything but shorts and sandals in an effort to keep more comfortable, and so it was, I remember, as we struggled in the blazing heat to turn that first field by hand. After a couple of hours, pouring with sweat and being maddened by flies, I found myself falling further and further behind and I began to realise that it's no good being too particular over the job, for that way you just don't cover the ground. Some sort of compromise has to be made between progress on the one hand

and thoroughness on the other, if the enormous undertaking is to get finished. Bill knew all about this from the start, of course, but it took me a long time to adapt my ways.

'Why didn't we get some cider for this job?' I shouted, as I began to wilt faster than the hay.

'Cider makes you sleepy!' returned Bill of the tireless fork. 'Water's much better. Go and get a can from the spring if you like.'

Bill had a quaint way of adding 'if you like' to his orders, even when he knew perfectly well I hated the prospect. 'You can hold her horns if you like!' he'd say about a cow whose hoof he was trying to inspect, or 'You can milk Jane tonight, if you like, while I have a go at that bad quarter of Violet's.'

Often enough I didn't 'like' but was too proud to object, even when I felt the action called for to be less than essential, as sometimes happened. But, on this occasion, I was only too glad to do the bidding and ran off down to the spring with a will. It's almost worth the discomfort of getting excessively hot and parched in the fields to experience the intense pleasure of a long cold drink, and I have known nothing – not even a longish cricket innings on a scorching day – to equal the over-heating that results from haymaking, old style, in a heatwave.

'We should be able to finish this by tea-time if we stick at it,' blinked Bill through the sweat running down his eyelids, when I handed him the can of water. 'We'd better not stop for lunch, though, but p'raps you could organise a sandwich or something to keep us going?'

'O.K. I'll see what I can do when I get to the end of this row. I never knew horse-flies hurt so much!' I said slapping at the four hundredth which had just made its presence felt on my left calf. 'But at least they're easier to kill than these ordinary brutes. Once they stick in their sharp proboscis, or whatever it is, they can't seem to escape quickly. I'm sure I've killed hundreds already!'

But Bill seemed impervious to the torture and wasn't prepared to waste talk on mere flies, so back I went to my post to resume acquaintance with my fork and cloud of buzzing tormentors. By sheer force of example Bill could always shame me into following his lead, however tough the going, as he did when I brought him up his sand-wich, and he scarcely stopped in his stride to grab it.

All through the afternoon we battled on and gradually the enemy was reduced to dwindling point, until we finally staggered down to the house for a late tea and a long sit-down to recover strength for the evening milking.

'And you mean to say one of these side-rake machines you talk about could do that job in a couple of hours?' I said weakly, with one eye on my blistered hands and some cooling in my ardour for the primitive methods.

'What chance of getting one for next year?'

'I could pick one up at a sale easily enough, but it wouldn't be much use without a tractor to pull it. Once we get a tractor we'll really be able to make some progress. I must have another word with Watkyn about it,' said Bill.

It is difficult to describe the mixed emotions of struggling through the chore of a late milking – which not infrequently turned out to be a 'midnighter' in harvest time – after a long day in the fields: a great sense of satisfaction at the day's achievements, on the one hand, mingling with an overwhelming feeling of fatigue, on the other. But it was certainly living in a sense the townsman scarcely knows. And we slept well o'nights.

Chapter 15

Help with the Hauling

The following day being a day of rest as far as the hay-field was concerned, while we waited for the continuing heatwave to work its wonders on our precious crop, we set about scrubbing out the interior of the Old Girl to make her fit for the all-important task of carrying in the harvest. Having been used for months as a pig and calf conveyor, to say nothing of fertilisers, feed-bags and cement, she called for a pretty thorough clean-up as cows have a powerful sense of smell and will spurn hay that has been in any way contaminated by contact. When we had sweetened up the interior as best we could, we left her with hood open to complete her ablutions in the blazing sunshine.

It was while this first field of hay was in process of 'making' that I was introduced to another charming little farm job that rears its head at this time of year: 'singling' the endless rows of roots and kale seedlings.

117

Our efforts in planting the steep field below the house were by this time showing a fine pay-off in the bright green mass of little plants which were growing almost fast enough to be a visible movement, and consequently Bill and I became human croquet hoops, bent double for days at a stretch while we moved up and down the rows at snails' pace. It struck me as crazy to be pulling up about ninety-nine per cent of our handiwork, as we were, just to give more room to the odd one in every foot or so, but Bill assured me it was the normal process and I imagine something of the sort is necessary if the seedlings aren't to choke themselves. Suffice it to say that 'singling' has remained a dirty word in my vocabulary ever since that first experience of it, and my back has never been quite the same again.

Surprisingly soon, thanks to the quite exceptional sunshine, Bill declared the hay ready to be made into 'cocks' for the carting operation. The technique here is to hold the butt of the pike against your stomach and simply slide along the swath, gathering hay like a snowball as you go. Of course, the hay has to be put into neat mounds which can be lifted cleanly when the time comes, but the sliding system speeds things up a lot, so that the whole field can be done in about half a day. I was surprised at the quantity of hay that goes into each cock, enough to call for a big effort to pick up at one go as I was to discover later. The damper rows near the hedges we left to benefit from a bit more sun the following morning, the plan being to start hauling after lunch on the morrow, when Gareth and Eirwen had promised to put in an appearance.

With our luck still holding in the matter of continuing fine weather, we completed the preparations next morning before going in for an early lunch, which we had scarcely finished before the approach of Eirwen and her brood made itself heard across the field from Bryncoed. Gareth wasn't far behind, carrying a well-worn pike and with shirt-sleeves rolled for action.

Bill and I went out to welcome them just as the kids scented fun and spread out to investigate our promising out-buildings. I was in time to see a tiny frock disappearing through the cowshed door so, while Bill fell to discussing plans with our cheerful helpers, I walked over to see what the kids were up to in the cowshed where we had a cow tied, waiting for a visit from the A.I. man.

When I looked in over the closed lower

half of the cowshed door, two funny little girls with matted hair were standing near Marigold, hand in hand.

'Hallo!' I said. 'And what are your names?' They continued to watch Marigold with keen interest but made no reply and I wondered if, perhaps, they were too young to speak.

'Are you talking to the pretty moo-cow?' I tried. One little girl pointed an accusing finger at the passive Marigold.

''Er's got the trots!' she declared.

'Oh? Ahem ... yes, I suppose so,' I faltered, rather taken aback.

'Our frocks get splashed and Mam gets cross. And Dad says bad words if he's got a clean shirt!' added the other girl, solemnly.

I would probably have learnt some more interesting titbits of information about life at Bryncoed if Eirwen's rallying call to her brood hadn't interrupted proceedings at that point and caused the little girls to scurry off back to the yard, still clasping one another's hands.

The kids, aided and abetted by their hearty Mum, were scrambling into the old taxi as Bill prepared to move off up to the hayfield and, looking a bit like a mobile version of the old woman's shoe in the nursery rhyme, with children peering out from all vantage points, it started up the track. Gareth and I followed on foot to join them for the first load.

By the time we caught up with the car, Eirwen had despatched her rowdy bunch, none of whom seemed to be more than about two, to a distant corner of the hayfield where they were already diving in amongst our carefully constructed haycocks and spreading them round once more. But the moment we had been waiting for was upon us and the first half-dozen forkfuls were slammed into the gaping back of the old car before Bill got aloft to tread it down and start to construct a proper load. With three of us pitching, Bill was hard-pressed to cope with all the hay arriving and it didn't take long before the interior was tightly crammed as far as the driver's partition and the load had reached the level of the roof.

The actual business of lifting the huge tumps of hay at one swoop was something I didn't always succeed in doing, unlike the lusty Eirwen who whisked the lot above her head as if it were a flag at the girl guides' outing. Like so many farm tasks, the business of achieving a stable load, even on a normal farm wagon or trailer, calls for a good deal of skill on the part of the chap on top. Although the pitcher does his best to place each massive forkful close against the previous one, it still has to be locked in tightly and adjusted for position, which only the loader is able to judge; and, above all, he must 'keep his middle filled', as the saying is, to ensure the whole load binds together and so avoid a disastrous loss en route to the hay barn. The upshot is that building a load was a tough job by any standards, the more so, of course, on a really hot day. The modern system of baling hay into convenient rectangular blocks, neatly tied with twine, has done away with both this loading job and its even tougher counterpart, the unloading. To achieve a stable load on the old car took some doing, but gradually it began to look like a mobile haystack as we tacked cautiously between the tumps with loud honks on the hooter as signals to Bill each time the car moved on.

By the time Bill called enough, the old taxi had virtually disappeared from sight, with hay to the running-boards, and even the driver's view almost blotted out completely. The chances of getting the towering load intact to the barn seemed pretty slight to me, but we were counting on Bill to get it there – I believe he could have coaxed the Old Girl up the side of Plynlimon if he's had a mind to and we set about roping it in professional fashion for the rough ride to the buildings. But if the trip down to the farmstead was tricky, the track leading from there to the barn was perilous, climbing through one of our roughest fields to approach the barn from the rear. While Bill edged the monstrous load jerkily up the rough track, Eirwen, Gareth and I stumbled alongside, supporting it as best we could from the lower side with our hayforks until, finally with much cheering, the last twist was safely negotiated to arrive alongside the empty barn.

'Marvellous old car!'

'I told you she'd make it.'

With the powerful Gareth throwing to Bill and me, the unloading was a lot quicker than the loading, at least in the early stages while the rick was below the level of the load.

By the time Eirwen had rounded up her brats from the many places of interest they had adjourned to around the farm, we were back among the haycocks, slowly reducing their number and transforming the Old Girl into a moving haystack once again. Having no cider to offer we were obliged to slake everyone's thirst with our precious beer, which did little to steady the ebullient Eirwen. Even the kids were given swigs from the flagon, right down to the youngest, rather to our surprise, but the job went on apace amidst much laughter and ribald comment.

'Might as well throw your trousers down, Gareth!' joked Eirwen, as her brawny husband shifted two or three massive tumps to every one of mine.

'Why d'you say that, then?' grunted Gareth.

'Well, you're working like a horse, so you might as well look like one!' she shrieked.

Load followed load in reaching the safety of the barn until, around seven o'clock, the last row of tumps finally fell to our forks and we drove down for a late tea, cock-a-hoop to have reached the end of the big job.

An egg each for the kids and two apiece for the adults, supported by stacks of bread and butter and enough cake to last us a month, were demolished while raucous laughter and lewd jokes filled the air, with no consideration given to the youthful ears all around. When I chanced to make some observation about the size of their family – there seemed to be kids everywhere – Gareth remarked that he'd be fattening up his wife again for Christmas, bringing on a deafening bout of laughter from the ample Eirwen sitting opposite. Bill's offer to lend him our old record of 'Night on the Bare Mountain' by way of mood music caused me a nasty choking fit and further gales of hilarity from our uninhibited guests.

Not till they'd cleaned us out of bread and cake did they think about calling it a day, but that was a small price to pay for the prodigious help they had given us, for we well knew that, but for them, we would scarcely have been half-way through the job and would certainly have been milking at midnight.

Chapter 16

'Some says Eyes and Some says Stomach!'

When we weren't tied up with our own hay, Bill and I would take turns to give a hand on neighbouring farms. This was how we came to meet up with some of our less immediate neighbours, and it gave us an amusing insight into the lives of these people. The day

I went over to help at a big, old-fashioned farm up on the higher land a mile or two north of our valley, was a case in point.

The system they used to get in the huge field was to have three large hay carts on the go constantly. No sooner was one wagon loaded, than another arrived empty from the hay barn. In similar fashion, the men working on the rick were kept busy with very short intervals between loads. Admirable organisation from the work study point of view, which Bill was always talking about, but not so good for the men who were obliged to keep up their effort almost non-stop right through the day. No time for a crafty fag between loads, which didn't please my mate on the pitching, none other than old Charlie, the Captain's tractor-man.

'I didn't expect to see you over here, Charlie,' I remarked while waiting for the tractor to draw on.

'Arrh!' replied Charlie, chattily.

'That field you ploughed for us is coming up a treat,' I tried again.

'I got the old 'eadache,' he said.

'Oh, Lord, have you really?' I sympathised. 'Not much fun with a headache in this weather.'

'I've always got the old 'eadache,' he went

on, warming to his subject.

'Can't you do anything for it?' I said. 'Aspirin or something?'

'There's nothing will touch it,' he declared, 'and no one can say the cause. Some says eyes and some says stomach!'

With this memorable remark, Charlie's conversation lapsed once more into little more than grunts. He was a morose sort of fellow, with a reputation for being cantankerous, but it seemed he had his reasons.

Another of the men helping in the field that day was a sprightly old chap with white hair. I was intrigued at the energy he showed for an 'old un', as he heaved up the heavy haycocks with no sign of effort. Unlike most of these Welsh countryfolk, he was quite gay and talkative, and I soon took to him.

'They tell me you boys is doing well at Vendre,' he remarked pleasantly. 'How would you like a slice of salmon for dinner one of these days?'

'Salmon! That sounds a bit of all right. How much d'you want for it?'

'I want the same as it costs,' he replied, 'and that's nothing because it's poached, you see!'

'Well, that's very kind of you, Mr … er…

Thank you very much.'

'Davey is the name – Davey Clydach. Right then, I'll drop some in for you tomorrow, I expect. Depending how we get on tonight, mind!'

'You mean you'll go fishing after a day's harvesting?' I gasped.

'Oh, yes. Just pitch into the milking when I get back and straight down to the river it is. We never miss our evening sport if we can help it. And it's better when it's raining, of course.'

Apart from my astonishment at the youthful vigour of the old chap, I was left wondering about his name. My guess was that it must be Mr Davey and Clydach his farm. I would have to ask Bill.

The chief snag, to my mind, about haymaking away from Vendre was the need to wear a shirt, proper trousers, shoes and socks, as distinct from the near nudity we practised in our own fields. Even so, I was almost indecently attired compared with the others. To 'throw down' anything more than their jackets was unheard-of, the standard dress being the black waistcoat, often complete with watch-chain, which never, under any circumstances, was removed. Underneath, the thickest woollen shirt and vest, albeit without collar, did duty with heavy corduroys, boots and woollen socks. Even in my flimsy shirt and slacks I had had more than enough of the heat by late afternoon when someone asked me to take over unloading in the barn to replace the cowman who had to go for milking.

It was a welcome relief to get under the shade of the multi-bay hay barn as the load was driven in and tucked close in alongside the rick. But I was glad I wasn't one of the two men up on the rick itself, close to the hot roof as they were, in the final stages of filling that particular bay. I recognised one of these fellows, a tough old character called Tom Wilkins, from the village. He had reputedly fought in the Boer War and was known to be a fine worker, but he rarely spoke at all except to say 'Aye, aye' to himself at regular intervals. His mate on the rick was a big fellow I didn't know, about half Tom's age and rather more genteel, if appearances were anything to go by.

Unloading a wagon of loose hay was one of the heaviest jobs on the farm in the days before baling made it obsolete. The trouble was that you'd be standing on part of the forkful of hay you were trying to lift, as often as not, with the obvious consequent strain on the stomach muscles. But, like so many farm jobs, it is not just brute strength that's called for: experience is half the battle. My mate on the wagon was the owner of the farm, and although a lot older than I was, he took some keeping up with. However, the ground gradually came nearer and our stretch more extended as we wrestled with our task. Eventually, we could see nothing of the two stalwarts above, except the ends of their extended hay-forks coming down out of the gloom to snatch our tip-toed offerings and whisk them out of sight.

In the final stages of filling the bay, old Tom and his mate were banking up the hay all round them to the roof, while working in an increasingly confined hollow, from which light and ventilation were being excluded. The heat and dust up there must have been intolerable and, eventually, the boss noticed that only one fork was coming down to take the hay each time, instead of two. He shaded his eyes in an effort to discern the shapes up above him in the gloomy hollow.

'Where's Mac then, Tom?' he shouted.

'Ewt!' came the unconcerned reply.

'Out! How d'ye mean, Tom?' returned the boss.

'Ewt!' repeated Tom, still busying himself

with the hay.

I had visions of poor Mac being covered over and entombed in the hayrick as the boss sprang into action. Sliding off the wagon, he quickly grabbed a ladder and hurried up to investigate, with me close behind. Sure enough, there was the huge form of Mac lying prostrate at the far side of the rick. He'd fainted off completely, which was hardly surprising, I thought, in that heat and dust. As I started off down the ladder again to fetch some water, old Tom was still putting the hay shipshape.

'Aye, aye,' he mumbled, with his usual half-smile and spitting on his hands by way of emphasis. 'Ewt, sure enough!'

These hay-making occasions always ended with a solemn rite known as 'Tea'. The host was honour-bound to provide a substantial meal, with the odd assortment of guests waited on by the womenfolk. The queer thing about these meals was that they took place in utter silence. It seemed to be taboo for anyone to speak a word, even to his neighbour, and the waiting women were similarly silent. Not until a man had finished, and signalled so by stacking his crockery and pushing it to the middle of the table, was he able to say a word. I imagine this is an old Welsh country custom, but I found it strange. Once the ritual of the dish-stacking has taken place, the guests light pipes and some desultory conversation breaks out until all have finished. At that point they all troop out with no attempt at thanks or farewells. But our efforts do not go unrewarded, for you will find a helper on your field next time you need one.

When I got back to Vendre I told Bill about the salmon offer.

'That must be the younger of the Clydach brothers,' he said. 'Clydach is a Forestry Commission holding way up on the bank across the valley, they tell me. A pretty tough place by all accounts.'

'Well, he looks as if he enjoys life,' I remarked, 'and he says they go fishing every evening, even after haymaking!'

'It must take them half an hour to reach the river from where they are, too. And steep going at that,' added Bill.

True to his word, Davey brought the salmon on the following day. I was mending a gap half-way up our lane when I saw his shock of white hair approaching on an old bike. Spotting me through the hedge as he passed, he waved cheerily and continued about a hundred yards down towards Vendre before coming to a halt against the bank. It wasn't till he turned and come back up to meet me that I realised why he hadn't stopped sooner. His bike was completely devoid of brakes; even the cables were missing!

'Here's two nice steaks each for you boys,' he began in his charming way, opening up an old leather shooting bag around his neck. 'Just fry them in butter, that's the best. No, no, I won't come in now, whatever. I wouldn't call against the table. But when are you coming up to see us at Clydach? Any time, any time. John and me will be very pleased to see you and give you a dish of tea. Just cross the little ford and straight up the track.'

When I put all this to Bill, he laughed.

'When does he think we'll find time, I wonder? That ford is as far as the road goes and we'd have a couple of miles' climb beyond there. Not much chance, I'm afraid.'

But if Davey had been trying to make a lifelong friend of himself, he was going the right way about it. I can still well-nigh taste the delicious salmon steaks he gave us, freshly caught and fried in butter as instructed. We ate them by themselves, ungarnished in any way and even Bill the fisherman, who had savoured many a fresh-caught trout, declared them perfect.

'Call 'against the table'? That's a new one,' said Bill. 'I suppose he meant it was about lunch-time. Ah, well, three cheers for John and Davey Clydach, I say!'

'Hear, hear!' I concurred, with feeling.

Chapter 17

Hot Weather Hazards

One of the few good things I ever read about the Chinese Communists was that they started a war on flies. Quite deliberately and methodically the insects and their breeding places were neutralised and, I believe, the results achieved were striking. Of course, we Europeans have done similar good work abroad against species like the mosquito and the tsetse fly, but the common 'house' fly has so far escaped any effort on the Chinese scale. In the countryside, the common fly is the blight of summer, slowly building up its power from a tolerable nuisance in the early stages to an infuriating climax in late July and August. To see cows and horses with their faces crawling with the things, and unable to knock them off, always upset me. We didn't have any sheep but they, of course, get it even worse when certain of the brutes bite the backs of their legs raw to lay their horrid eggs in the flesh.

I can remember one oppressive day when I was actually driven out of a field by flies, rather to my shame. I had gone down to weed the kale below the house in late July, by which time it was beginning to look a most impressive crop, having been singled at great cost in sweat and backache earlier in the year. The flies that day seemed possessed, and determined to eat me alive, and I was back on the yard in less than half an hour, explaining to a smiling Bill that the field was uninhabitable. With his usual magnanimity he accepted my story, but I felt a bit like King Daggerbear, in the old song, who was chased out of the wood by a rabbit.

It was to combat the flies in that long hot summer that we put the cows down in the bottom meadow, the scene of the duck-shooting miracle, where the surrounding copses offered them plenty of shade and protection. The snag about using that meadow and SNAG it certainly was, lay in the fact that access to it was only possible through a veritable morass, stretching about thirty yards at its narrowest point. It is no exaggeration to say that the cows sank to their 'armpits' in what soon became a sea of mud, so that they dragged themselves through it on their bellies with a front leg action reminiscent of a swimmer doing the crawl. Strangely enough, the only cow ever to get completely stuck was the rather feeble little Jersey cross, Denise, who had to be ignominiously hauled out by Gareth's horse on one occasion. For the most part, the cows simply waded in happily enough, to struggle heavily out at the other side, under-sealed with pure clay. As for the human element in bringing them through, it was possible to navigate without sinking into the deeper parts, though a considerable effort was called for, involving the not infrequent loss of rubber boot, retrieved by balancing act in arrear, as it were.

The Slough of Despond, as we soon came to know it, was doubly unfortunate in its consequences. In the first place it rendered the comparatively small task of getting in the cows of an evening into something of a major operation, enough to take the edge completely off what little energy one still had left by that time after a hot day. It took a good forty minutes to retrieve them from the meadow, urge them through the Slough, and bring them up the steep field, uncomfortably hot in one's gumboots, to their ties in the cowshed. But worse was to follow – much worse! Cows' udders are always washed before milking and it was here that the bog really made its presence felt, for the job of getting off that caked mud, completely smothering their 'bags' as it did, would call for two or three buckets of water per cow, not to mention the effort and time that went into it. With a freshly calved cow, in particular our seven-galloner, Jane, whose mine-like udder almost touched the ground, the washing alone could take ten minutes, adding upwards of an hour to the routine job of milking. The last straw was sitting squashed between the heaving stomachs for the actual milking, with one's final ounce of energy being sapped by the unwelcome heat. I think it was that summer-time experience that put the tin lid on hand-milking in my estimation. It's the nearest thing to purgatory I've ever experienced.

'I wish to blazes we had a milking machine,' I used to moan frequently.

'Well, we can't afford one,' was Bill's standard reply. 'With no electricity, it would mean an engine to drive it as well as all the rest, vacuum pump, piping and buckets. It would cost a bomb, and there are lots of things we need more urgently.'

But, all credit to Bill, he bore the great weight of the milking while I continued to struggle with a few of the easier cows. And he never complained, amazingly enough. I must be a sap, I used to tell myself, making a fuss about nothing.

'Watkyn says we can have a couple of his old TVO tanks for a pound apiece,' said Bill one day in August. 'With that big water tank of ours we'll then be able to start the whey idea before the winter sets in.'

'At what age can pigs start having whey?' I queried.

'As soon as they're weaned at eight weeks or so, they can go straight on to it. We could start with this latest batch in about a fortnight.'

'We should be able to save a lot on pig meal, then?'

'Oh, yes, it's miles cheaper than meal and apparently they can be fattened on whey alone, but that seems a bit drastic,' said Bill. 'I think we'll have to change over gradually and just see how it goes.'

We duly brought over the two paraffin tanks, one at a time, in the Old Girl, and set about washing them out as best we could before placing them on wooden stands along the lower edge of the yard where the tanker could easily pump out its contents.

'The minimum order they'll take is for a thousand gallons,' explained Bill. 'It works out at about three-halfpence a gallon, incredibly cheap when you think it includes transport from the cheese factory.'

When the first load arrived, however, we were amused to find the young pigs didn't think much of the whishy-washy liquid. They would stick their snouts into it and blow bubbles in disgust, making no attempt to drink the stuff.

'Well, they'll have to learn to like it,' said Bill. 'The next thousand gallons is due a fortnight today!'

In the early stages we gave alternate feeds of meal and whey. Probably because of the cut-back in their solid food, the manners of the porkers at the trough worsened rather strikingly. It became next to impossible to spread the meal along the trough before the frantic customers dived in feet and all. I grew exasperated at the speed and force with which my feed bucket was knocked askew while trying to achieve an even spread for all to share, and on one occasion, which I've never been able to live down, Bill was astonished to see a half-grown porker come sailing out of the door's open top half, to land heavily in some bushes several yards beyond. I had resorted to violence again in un-farmer-like fashion. Ironically, those same pigs got their own back shortly afterwards. In the struggle to serve their repast I had removed my jacket and thrown it over the wooden partition, the pigs had found it and had it for 'afters', complete with the contents of the pockets!

'What was in it altogether?' enquired a laughing Bill as he helped me search the dark recesses of the mucky pen later that evening.

'My fountain pen, for a start,' I said. 'Oh! and my pipe – the one with the silver band I'm so fond of.'

There was no trace whatsoever of the jacket, not so much as a wisp of cloth, but we persevered in our search as I was quite sure where I'd left it. Eventually I trod on something hard which turned out to be the pipe's bowl, much chewed and devoid of any stem. Of the pen we could find no trace, but there was a remarkable sequel for, more than six months later while taking out the muck in the early spring, Bill's sharp eyes spotted something glinting in the midden. It turned out to be the gold nib, apparently undamaged, together with the plastic filler-mechanism to which it was attached, the outer shell and screw-on cap having disappeared. After washing it in the strongest disinfectants from the dairy I sent it back to the makers to see if they could replace the missing barrel and cap. This they did, and the pen functioned as well as ever but, notwithstanding all the disinfectants, it retained its pungent smell as a permanent remainder of its six-month sojourn in a manure heap.

For me there was one other happy outcome of the demise of my jacket: Bill declared that the farm account would pay for a new pipe to replace the one the pigs had eaten. And the simple pleasure of buying myself something new, at a time when neither of us spent a penny that wasn't essential to the furtherance of farm interest, cheered me a lot and was a boost to my morale. It was a kind thought of Bill's and much appreciated at the time.

Chapter 18

A Fine Crop of Thistles

Old Kropje, the Latvian, had decided that year to show the valley a thing or two by growing a field of wheat, not a common practice by any means in that high-rainfall area of central Wales. So, one hot afternoon in August I drove down to lend a hand with the stooking, parking the Old Girl at the bottom of Kropje's awful lane and walking up under the overhanging banks where he almost met his Waterloo on more than one occasion.

As I approached the broken-down buildings of the farmstead I noticed, to my surprise, a fine crop of thistles surrounding the place, with seeds floating everywhere on the light summer breeze. It wasn't till I'd joined Kropje and his helpers in the field, though, that I appreciated their full significance: the sheaves were riddled with the things.

'Is good for ze rheumatism!' shouted my host, encouragingly, when he saw me stopping at regular intervals to examine my punctured fingers. 'Many thistles means a mild vinter, too.'

'How about the summer after next?' I countered, feeling a bit short of temper at the agonies I was suffering.

'You laugh at me, but it ees as I say. You veel see!'

I didn't argue the toss but decided to bring gloves another time, whatever the locals might think.

The business of putting up corn sheaves, in pairs, to make stooks of eight, standing on their butt-ends so as to give the grain every chance to ripen during the three weeks or so it used to remain out, is now a thing of the past as far as I know. The long-serving 'binder', which cut and tied the corn in sheaves, such a great advance on the older techniques of scything and tying by hand, has long since given way to the combine harvester, the huge and costly machine which eliminates sheaves altogether and all the odd jobs associated with them. Undoubtedly it is a tremendous advance, cutting out all the old worries of losing the crop to the weather after cutting, as well as doing away with the separate job of threshing later on, but it's a bit sad that all the delights of the harvest field, the high-spot of the country people's social calendar for so long, should have been lost at the same time.

I hadn't been working long before I saw a tractor draw up at the farm and two more helpers get off and head in our direction. As they came nearer I could see that one of these men was a weird and hideous-looking individual with a strange ape-like gait and wearing an old army greatcoat buttoned up to the neck, despite the hot weather. After a word with Kropje he tottered in my direction, with his right hand held out in front of his face and croaking something incomprehensible as he approached.

Resisting a strong urge to turn and run, I eventually caught the words, 'That much!', and realised he was indicating a small distance of about half an inch with his outstretched finger and thumb.

'Wh ... what?' I stammered.

'That much!' he repeated, huskily. 'That's all the room you left us!'

At last the penny dropped and I grasped that he was referring to the Old Girl at the bottom of the lane, which the tractor had evidently been hard pressed to get past.

'Oh, I'm sorry,' I faltered. 'I hadn't expected any traffic to use that lane.'

'Ay, that much!' he repeated, by way of emphasis. 'That's all you left us, indeed!'

How was I to know this frightening-looking fellow was one Willy John, a harmless simpleton who worked a smallholding with his brother a few miles out of the valley? He had been brought over by his neighbour, the tractor owner, to swell the numbers, and evidently Kropje had decreed he was to be my 'mate' on the stooking job, hardly the one I would have chosen from the conversational point of view. However, his aggressive manner soon gave way to broad grins as he saw me trying to squeeze out thistles, something he seemed wholly impervious to, judging by the way he grabbed the sheaves and jammed them into place in the stooks.

'You just put up the ones without thistles,' he said, after a bit. 'Leave the bad ones for me, isn't it?'

'That's very kind of you, Mr ... er. Thank you very much.'

'Plenty of brains with me, Mr Barnett,' he winked, grabbing the most frightful thistles as if they were ragwort. 'Yes, indeed, plenty of brains with me!'

And so we worked on through the hot afternoon, with Willy John seizing all the worst sheaves before I had time even to consider them, and I making an effort to be affable in recognition of his kindness. Despite his permanent leer and compulsive winkings I gradually came to feel less apprehensive and to realise he was a well-meaning fellow, anxious to please. Even so, he was the nearest thing to a nut case I met in my farming experience and I suspect it was only the kindliness of the people of those parts that kept him out of an institution.

When the stooking was at last finished and we had had a cup of tea and suffered a few more snippets of weather lore from old Kropje, I found myself walking down the lane towards the car with Willy John still sticking like a limpet.

'Can I give you a lift home?' I said, the tractor owner having gone before tea and Willy evidently left to his own devices.

'That would be very kind. Thank you. Yes, very kind, indeed!'

So off we set in the taxi, up a narrow road a mile or two out of the valley to the south-ward.

My plan of just dropping off my passenger and returning the way I'd come, however, was immediately thwarted by the elder brother, Dai John, who was standing by the gate of their small-holding as we drew up, looking like the original one eyed giant. About twice the size of the younger Willy, this fellow lacked the stoop and the facial contortions of his brother, but made an even more striking impact with his massive physique, allied to a completely expressionless face and a brow like Pithecanthropus himself.

'COME IN! COME IN!' he boomed, ignoring my protests about being late for milking. 'You must see what I'm doing in the house: just putting in a new washbasin, indeed.'

I followed meekly down the garden path, with Willy John shuffling behind, though my instinct was against going anywhere with these two madmen.

'There now! What d'you think of that?' said Cyclops, with obvious pride, as he showed me into the living-room to see a wash-basin slap in the middle of the floor space.

'My word, yes, that's a beauty!' I mumbled, finding words a bit hard to come by. As far as I could see it would simply have to be filled with a bucket and emptied by the same method. I imagine they were so thrilled to have a modern wash-basin that the question of plumbing didn't come into the reckoning.

'Come on through to the kitchen and see

what I'm doing there,' boomed Dai when I'd exhausted my praise of the wash-basin. From there we proceeded to the garden and greenhouses, all shown with the greatest pride and calling for endless words of approval on my part. By the time I escaped to the taxi I was thoroughly exhausted, though not a little relieved to have come out alive.

In one respect, though, the John brothers were not as crazy as they looked, for as a result of my mentioning that we grew no vegetables one of them would call regularly with a selection from their garden, and the price was always the same as the shop charged, about double what they would have got from the wholesale merchants.

Chapter 19

Six Acres for Silage

The Captain turned up trumps once again by lending us his little Ferguson tractor and trailer-plough in early September, so that we might plant a crop for silage the following year. As with so many other aspects of my new life, I was a complete novice regarding the whole operation and was intrigued to learn the extent of the work and expense required to produce a simple crop, even using up-to-date machinery as we did for a large part of the job. I hate to think how much time and effort must have been called for in these operations before the tractor replaced the team of horses.

The plan was to sow the big field next to the road to a mixture of peas and oats, good stuff, Bill assured me, for silage making. I gathered that the crop would be cut and carted in green condition, with none of the dependence on fine weather that most crops called for, thrown off into a deep pit in the ground, covered over with earth and left to heat up and preserve itself in the acids produced. Sometimes a solution of molasses is sprinkled on to assist the processes, but it isn't essential and Bill didn't propose to bother with it.

'That's a nice little treat in store for us, too!' he said, with one of his nasty hollow laughs. 'Digging the silage pit, I mean.'

'Hmm! And when do you reckon to do that?'

'In the spring, I suppose. I'll have to get some advice from the Ministry on siting it, but we shan't need it till June, so there's no hurry.'

We were going to borrow all the implements for the job from the Captain, except for the wide, box-like seed drill, with little shutes that convey the seed down into the soil. Apparently the gateway into the field was too narrow for the drill, so Bill spent a few pounds on a second-hand 'fiddle', an amusing device that sprays out seed when the operator pushes a bow-like activating stick through it in the fashion of a violin player.

'The fiddle is best for grass seed, but it should do the oats all right,' explained Bill, when he brought it in one evening. 'The peas will have to be broadcast by hand, though, and so will the fertilisers.'

Our taciturn neighbour, Charlie, had already dumped an assortment of heavy implements, including a roller, in the six-acre field when he eventually brought the tractor over according to plan.

'I've just dropped the "two-furrow" by the gate,' he grunted as he started off across the fields towards his cottage on foot. 'The Governor says you can 'ave it till Thursday.'

'Fair enough, Thursday it is then,' returned Bill. 'Thanks, Charlie.'

I had never seen a 'Fergy' at close quarters before, so Bill spent a bit of time explaining how everything worked, bearing in mind that I was to be relief tractor driver for the next two days, this being Monday.

'Just what we could do with, one of these!' I remarked, full of admiration for the compact little machine, so different from other tractors of the day. 'How much are they?'

'About three hundred quid, I believe. We certainly haven't got the work to justify that sort of outlay, even if we had the money to spare. But I'll tell you something: Watkyn thinks he may be able to resurrect an ancient Massey he's come across. That would give us a tractor – of sorts – for a tenth of the price.'

'Has he really? That's good news! Good old Watkyn,' I said, 'but I bet it doesn't compare with this little beauty.'

'Well, no,' admitted Bill. 'It's much bigger, for a start, and I believe it's got steel wheels on the front. But the engine's damaged and Watkyn hasn't had time to strip it down yet, so we'll just have to keep our fingers crossed.'

'Ah, well, here's hoping!'

'Right, then, action stations! Start ploughing at five, so early night tonight!' ordered Bill, with the glint of battle in his eye.

Long before dawn Bill was stirring. He was hoping to get in a couple of hours' ploughing before having to break off for the milking, when I would take over for a spell.

'You won't be able to see what you're doing – it's still pitch dark outside,' I grumbled. But, as I was to find out in the course of time, Bill took some holding when he had the bit between his teeth, and before long I heard the tractor start with a splutter and roar off up the lane.

By the time I had found the willpower to crawl out, had my early cup of tea, got the cows in and milked my old friend Hyacinth, Bill had been at it for a good two hours. As I trotted up the lane I could see a sizeable patch of dark brown showing up in stark contrast to the rest of the pale field.

'It looks good!' I yelled above the tractor's noise. 'How d'you keep the furrows so straight?'

'Nothing to it as long as you keep the front wheel tucked in against the previous cut,' shouted Bill.

Like most of his 'nothing to it' jobs, it took some getting hold of, the trickiest part being to lift out the plough to turn at the 'headlands' and lower it again by a deft pull on its string at the crucial moment to start the next pair of furrows. The tractor needed to be steered with the greatest accuracy just as one's head was turned to let down the plough. I had a nasty feeling I was giving Evans-the-Road some good anecdotal material in the odd patterns I was producing on these turns, but hoped Bill might be able to straighten out, or hide, the worst before the populace had time to see it.

Time plays strange tricks, I was to discover, when working on a field scale. The hours tend to slip by almost unnoticed. The cause, I suspect, is a combination of two factors, the concentration called for the whole time if one is to avoid irremediable errors, on the one hand, and the sheer size of each unit of the task, on the other. One tends to think of each traverse of the field as a tiny unit of the whole, forgetting that it is about a furlong in length and therefore of several minutes' time equivalent.

By the time Bill reappeared he had not only milked the cows and turned them out but had his breakfast as well. The half-hour that I imagined I'd been driving for was, in fact, nearer two hours.

'Good work!' yelled Bill. 'I should be able to finish, except for the headlands, by lunchtime. I'll be down on the tractor about one,

I expect.'

When the time came, Bill was in no mood to waste any of it in eating. He snatched a few mouthfuls and was off again to do battle with the headlands, the farmer's name for the unploughed patches at either end of the field which have to be left for turning purposes. I followed him shortly on foot to see the operation and give a hand with the change-over to the disc harrows which would follow.

I hadn't realised before what a hammering a tractor must take. Not only does it have to keep going all day at busy seasons, but the buffeting it gets from the roughness of a ploughed field would soon shake a less robust vehicle to bits. Discing of the ploughed field is considerably rougher even than the ploughing, for now the tractor is rather like a ship at sea, sailing out across the furrows, and plunging into innumerable troughs. The implement known as 'the discs' is, in fact, a heavy set of sharp metal wheels, perhaps a foot in diameter, which are drawn across the newly ploughed field to cut the furrows into lumps which can then more easily be broken down by the spike harrows into the fine tilth necessary for sowing seed into. Discing is an altogether quicker business than the ploughing, since the width of the discs is about three times that of the two furrow plough, while harrowing is quicker still as the tractor is then driven in a higher gear – just about flat out when Bill was doing it – to hasten the breaking down of the more obstinate lumps.

'It's broken down quite well,' said Bill at about tea-time, when we had both had enough of the tractor's roar. 'It won't need rolling, but I think an hour or two with the chain harrows in the morning should just about do it.'

'What can the chain harrows do that this one can't?' I asked, looking at the metal jig-saw still attached to the Fergy.

'It hasn't got spikes like this one to tear into the topsoil,' explained Bill patiently as we started for home. 'It rattles loosely over the surface to give a finer finish.'

'So, apart from that, we're all set to start sowing tomorrow?'

'Yes, that's where the fun will be,' returned Bill. 'It should be interesting!'

The first thing to be done next morning was to load up the old taxi with fertilisers. Most of this was in hundredweight bags and I was a bit aghast to see how many were set aside for this one field.

'The recommended dose is four hundred-weight of phosphates to the acre,' explained Bill. 'That's twenty-four bags. Then two tons of lime to the acre and we should have plenty to keep us out of mischief.'

'Two TONS!' I gasped. 'There isn't that much here altogether.'

'No, true enough, there's only thirty bags here which will be better than nothing, but nowhere near the recommended dose. We'll have to put some more on later.'

Considering we were proposing to put it all on the field a handful at a time, I wasn't sorry to hear the dose was being curtailed.

'We'll need a bucket each to carry it in, of course,' Bill went on, 'and our old friend the fiddle for the corn.'

So we loaded up the Old Girl with as much as we thought she could safely take and set off for the field once more. After the long dry summer the soil was very friable and the tilth already seemed pretty good to me. All the same, I was soon aboard the Fergy, towing the lighter chain harrows at a rate of knots, while Bill busied himself pacing out the edges and weighing the seed into old sacks he'd brought for the purpose.

By mid-morning we had started on the big

job, Bill with his bucket of seed being serenaded close behind by my violin. I found it hard to stop laughing in the early stages at the comical figures we were cutting, with Bill striding jerkily to maintain his rhythm while I fiddled for all I was worth. Fortunately, there were only the birds to laugh as we marched idiotically up and down the field. Bill's great right arm swings seemed to be making a good spread from my vantage point but, as he soon pointed out, it's next to impossible to cover the ground evenly with that system. The fiddle certainly achieves a more even spread but soon begins to feel a dead weight, supported under one arm, as it is. Bill's careful weighing operations had not been in vain, for the seed panned out surprisingly accurately and, after about two hours of march and counter-march, the whole field had got its sprinkling.

'We'll soon see what sort of a mess we've made of it when the seeds begin to shoot,' laughed Bill. 'They should be showing in a couple of weeks. I'll harrow it now to cover over the seeds and it will help to keep the birds off till we've had some lunch. That'll give us the afternoon for the fertilisers. Hope you're feeling strong!'

By the time I had rejoined him after lunch

and one or two farm chores, Bill had got the artificials opened and ready to start.

'You'd better do the phosphates,' he said. 'The lime is going to be difficult. Just look at it!'

'It looks mostly dust,' I said. 'Better you than me!'

'It's supposed to be only a tenth dust, by weight, so nine-tenths should go to ground, even if the other tenth gets breathed in. A bit of lime is good for you, anyway, not like some of the chemicals they're producing for crops nowadays.'

'This breeze should blow it away from you,' I said encouragingly.

I soon found, when we started marching once more, that my phosphate granules also contained a fair bit of dust for inhalation purposes. The difficulty is to take the same sized fistful at each step, there being no time to adjust if one is to keep the swing in unison with the stride, and a long throw is called for rather than a short one if there is to be any sort of an even coverage. Bill was soon lost in a white cloud which drifted slowly across towards the road.

We'd been at this part of the job for an hour or so when Kropje suddenly appeared waving over the hedge at the roadside.

'IS TOO MUCH VIND FOR LIMING TODAY!' he shouted when Bill and I stopped in our tracks. 'IS PITY TO THROW MONEY OVER ZE HEDGE!'

'I'll throw him over the hedge if he isn't careful!' growled Bill in my direction, while giving Kropje a non-committal wave.

'I AM MANY YEARS FARMING AND VISH TO HELP YOU', persisted the tactless Kropje. 'IS BETTER TO PUT ON OWN FARM AND NOT ZE NEIGHBOUR'S!'

He was still labouring the point when Bill resumed his march, cloud aloft. Kropje soon took the hint and went on his way while Bill and I continued our mechanical doll act till well into the evening. I was heartily tired of hugging the bucket long before we got through all the bags of phosphate, and my right arm was aching from the constant swinging. As usual my enthusiasm for doing things the basic way was giving way a little to the advantages of mechanisation.

'How are these artificial applied nowadays, then?' I queried as we collected up the paper sacks at the finish.

'Lime is usually spread direct from lorries built for the job,' replied Bill, 'but the others are drilled in or spread by a spinning device behind a tractor.'

'Just think what this field has cost to seed,' I said. 'Thirty quid's worth of seeds, did you say, and how much for the fertiliser?'

'At least twenty if we include the rest of the lime it will need, but we only pay half, thanks to the subsidy.'

'Well, even so, that's forty pounds, plus TVO for the tractor, not to mention the hard work and the capital outlay on machinery. And all that for six acres – I wouldn't like to finance a really big field.'

We were late to bed that night. The batteries have to be re-charged with a sit-down and something to eat before you can undertake another big job such as milking, and by the time we crawled off up the ladder we were both ready to drop, but somehow elated to have done battle with Mother Earth herself and put up a fair showing.

Chapter 20

Potato-picking Days

By the time that unusually fine summer had given way to the cold, but still sunny, days of early autumn, our steep field of cultivations, below the house, was coming on apace. The kale, in particular, had exceeded our wildest dreams and, so far from growing into large cabbages as Bill had forecast, it began to look more like a forest of palm trees.

'Some of those plants are taller than I am,' I told him one day, after taking a stroll down to look at them, 'and the stems are as thick as cricket bat handles.'

'We'll have to start feeding a bit soon,' returned Bill, 'but most of it will be growing for another month or two yet. It's going to be quite a crop by the time it's finished.'

'Well, that should give the locals something to think about,' I chortled. 'It just shows what can be done with a bit of know-how.'

'FYM would be nearer the mark. It should be better still with all this pig muck next year. If we can ever pick it up, that is.'

Bill had touched on a sore point. My pride and joy, the midden, had been resisting my efforts to achieve the fine design of the previous year ever since we'd started feeding whey. It had lately developed an alarming tendency to spread out sideways, and the prospect of wet weather to come was one we preferred not to think about.

Like ourselves, old Kropje had a crop of potatoes to harvest, and Bill and I took in it turns to lend a hand in the lifting which spread over several days as it was a lot more extensive than ours. Unlike so many farm jobs, potato picking is really very pleasant, with bulging sacks to show for one's efforts and no exterior factors such as flies or excessive heat to take the gilt off the gingerbread. Given some normal autumn sunshine the job can make a very pleasant interlude and so, for the most part, it proved on Kropje's farm. The system used was for Kropje to run his little tractor down the rows towing Gareth's ancient plough-like device which had to be wrestled with in the manner of the horse ploughman steering his furrow. As if by magic, the field is sprayed with fine white potatoes which are then simply gathered my as many helpers as may chance to turn up.

Gathering the spuds is an easy and satisfying job, if liable to give one backache after a few hours.

One queer fellow who was helping there was introduced to me by Kropje as 'Mr Jones'. When I got a chance, I asked Kropje who this fellow Jones was, since it was an extremely common name and one liked to know something about one's colleagues, if only for future reference.

'Mr Jones,' condescended Kropje, weighing his words carefully, 'is ze husband of Mrs Jones.' It was no wonder that Bill, who saw a lot more of him than I did, never really took to the Latvian.

When Kropje's field was finished he brought the ancient implement over to Vendre to help us lift our own potatoes. Unfortunately the weather was beginning to break by this time and the day we chose was one of those bright, showery days which can't be trusted for long. With Bill on the 'plough', Kropje ran his tractor down the first steep row while I took the sacks to the bottom of the field before we all started gathering, working uphill against the slope so as to reduce the amount of stooping required. Before long the first shower arrived to make things a bit sticky, but we worked on through it without undue concern. Perhaps observing his lack of impact, the weatherclerk decided to let go with all he'd got not long afterwards: rain and hail, with icy wind in support. Very soon, little rivulets were running down the field and I waited expectantly for the word from Bill to adjourn to the buildings till the shower should subside. But the word did not come. Bill was keeping his head down as if nothing were amiss. Neither Kropje nor I could break the convention by suggesting a withdrawal, such a course being the entire prerogative of the farmer on whose land one worked, by some unwritten law of the countryside. Even when the force of the downpour had made it difficult to keep our footing on the slippery slope, our fingers were quite numb and our jackets had given up their attempt to keep the rain out, we still worked on with never a word between us. I decided to give Bill a piece of my mind as soon as I got a chance.

'Why the hell didn't you call it off in that deluge?' I wailed when Kropje had gone. 'That's the last time I'm working in that sort of rain.'

'Call it off?' said Bill, incredulous. 'And let old Crapper off the hook? Talk sense, man!'

As the autumn wore on towards Christmas, I came to know the slippery propensities of that field very well indeed. It somehow became my job to descend every afternoon, as dusk approached, armed with machete and large sheet of sacking, to get the evening's ration of kale for the milkers. However hard I tried to avoid getting sluiced in icy water down my neck from the large head-high leaves, it always happened sooner or later, rather like hoping not to get stung while cutting nettles with a hook. But, if the chopping down and stacking of my load on the spread sacking had its little hazards, they were not to be compared with the perils of the return to base. To swing the huge swag bag over my shoulder, weighing the better part of a hundredweight as it did, was just a preliminary to the main task of tacking up the slithery field, like Atlas with the world on his shoulders, to regain the yard. Invariably I would slip to one knee in the mud and occasionally even drop the whole burden, but I was always spurred on by the thought of the pleasure and benefit the cows got from the stuff. They really relished it, especially when the grass was finished, and would snatch it from my grip in their delight. The tough stems were reduced to pulp in no time and it was made abundantly clear that I should have brought twice as much. Little did they know! I always kept a few choice bits for my particular friend, Minnie Mouse, whose way of saying 'Thank you' was to snatch it even more violently than the others. But the look in her eye, I could tell, was highly appreciative.

The long, dark evenings having come round again we decided a general stocktaking of our situation was very much overdue. We seemed to have been out and about all day and every day, ever since the break-up of the long frost had heralded the superb summer, and it was high time to have another of our 'financials', to see how things were really going.

The upshot of our deliberations when we eventually got round to them, was not encouraging. Taking into account the money we owed the feed merchants, who always permitted a good deal of credit, it seemed that our capital was almost gone. To add up all we had bought, at least the cost of the major items, nothing like accounted for what we'd spent; but the bank statements were clear enough and the money had gone somewhere. Bill had recently laid out at least a hundred on four in-calf heifers which wouldn't show any return till the spring, and there were now five calves, all costing money to rear and likewise unproductive at present.

On the pig side of the enterprise, we had bought two Wessex saddleback sows way back in the summer, and spent a good deal on improvements to the fattening pens to cope with the increased porkers. We'd also pumped a lot of fertiliser into the land in the hope of future returns. On the other hand, we had bought no machinery at all except an electric fence, we spent next to nothing on entertainment and we lived pretty frugally by any standards.

'It seems to me,' pronounced Bill at length, 'that next spring will be the turning point. They always say, in farming, that it's getting established that costs the money, and that's what's happened in our case. But with all this new stock coming on, the increase in milk and porkers should swing the balance after about Lady Day.'

'Well, at least we won't have any expenses between now and then,' I put in. 'Except that we ought to get that tractor, of course.'

'That's true. No stock to buy, no cultivations, no money out on the buildings and I don't propose spending more than a hundred on tractor and trailer, at the very outside. It will be rather marvellous, really, if we can turn the corner and become a viable business without going into the red.'

'Hasn't Watkyn come up with anything in the way of a tractor yet?' I queried. 'What about that old Massey he found somewhere?'

'No luck, I'm afraid. He's decided the engine's beyond repair, so we're back to square one. If he hasn't found anything by about February, I'll have to see what I can do at the spring sales,' sighed Bill, putting all the papers away. 'Heavens, look at the time! Come on! The milking!'

Chapter 21

Yard Awash!

The New Year, which was to be the one when we progressed out of the Wheelbarrow Era, started with something of a fright for both of us. We had crawled off to bed in good time on New Year's Eve, after declining one or two invitations to see the New Year in, and were making the most of our limited dream-time when the pervading silence of the winter night was shattered by a short, sharp, staccato noise which brought us back to consciousness with a bump. We were both lying still, blinking and trying to decipher the sound we'd heard when it came again like a clarion call to make our hair stand on end. It took a moment or two, with beating hearts, for our sleep-fuddled brains to recognise the sound for what it was: nothing less than a Welsh choir in full voice letting go the four syllables of 'HAP/PY/NEW/YEAR!', complete with all the descants and harmonies of which they are capable. After a further silence of perhaps half a minute, a third crystal-clear harmonic blast rent the air, and then no further sound at all, no banging on the door, no sound of footsteps, but only Trigger's desultory barking in the distance. It was all so eerie it might have been a phantom choir, had it not been for the many footprints we found in the snow next morning. We never did find out who our visitors had been but assumed it was some well intentioned singers who roamed the country unaware, perhaps, that their form of greeting was enough to give its recipients heart failure.

Nor was that the only time I was brought back from the Land of Nod that winter, for one night Bill heard Gertie on the point of smothering one of her babes, a little trick she did from time to time, unlike her more intelligent sister, Elsie. The muffled squeal was a sound Bill knew well and, without a thought for his sleeping partner, he let fly an enormous roar.

'GERTIE ... YOU OLD BASTARD' emanating fortissimo from the darkness alongside, brought me to the sitting-up, hair-on-end position like a Punch and Judy doll. Some idea of the power of the shout can be gleaned from the fact that the squealing stopped immediately despite our being a good fifty yards from Gertie's sty and in a room with tiny, closed windows.

It was this same litter of Gertie's which produced our first runt, a poor little chap barely half the size of his brothers and sisters, and distinctly seedy-looking.

'It's no good keeping it,' explained the practical Bill. 'It will never do any good and just be a waste of food. I'd better shoot it!'

'Oh, we can't kill the poor little thing!' I protested. 'P'raps we can give it away to Kropje or someone?'

'I doubt if anyone would want it, but I'll ask around if you like,' agreed Bill.

The first person to come and take a look

at it was Evans-the-Road who came down to the farm after Bill had mentioned it to him earlier in the day, but he soon decided it was not for him.

'It's too small to fatten properly, you understand,' he explained, 'but I'll take one of these others off you, whatever. I like to have a pig for the household scraps – and I kill and cure it myself, you see,' he added, licking his chops in pointed fashion.

Kropje also declined the offer but, to our surprise, Gareth said that Eirwen would take it and bring it up by hand. So we duly handed over the little runt to make one less for Gertie to have to worry about and, a few weeks later, when Bill went over to see Gareth about something, he was astonished to find the pig living in the kitchen like a pet dog, and sharing quarters with Eirwen's latest addition, a baby girl of barely twelve months. Whether she used the same bottle to feed it or not we never found out, but considered it a distinct possibility.

When Gertie's litter was weaned, at eight weeks old, I undertook to drop off Evans-the-Road's pig on a trip to the village.

'There'll be a bit for you and your brother,' grimaced Evans, as he licked his chops again at the thought. 'I'm not saying when, mind, but you'll be having a nice piece of ham, whatever.'

The new sows that I had watched Bill bid for at Welshpool pig market in the summer, being 'Saddlebacks' – black fore and aft with a wide white band round the middle – were intended to produce porkers rather than baconers. By crossing the Saddleback sows with a Large White boar we got what are called 'blue spot' progeny, suitable as either porkers or baconers, so we were able to ring the changes as circumstances dictated. Porkers, too, are normally ready for slaughter at least one month earlier than their bacon cousins, which gave us a quicker turnover and cash return.

We christened these two sows 'Gorg' and 'Zola' on account of their extraordinary partiality for whey, something that Elsie and Gertie disapproved of strongly. The piglets, with their funny markings like so many little uniforms, were even more intriguing, I thought, than the Large Whites. But the net result was to double the number of pigs being fattened at any one time and the principal feature of that second winter was the interminable carrying of buckets of whey from the tanks at the bottom of the yard to the fattening pens at the top. Right through those winter months we fed a thousand gallons a fortnight, five hundred a week or seventy-one a day, and I came to feel like the broom in Disney's version of the Sorcerer's Apprentice. And it all had to be carried up a one in four slope before breakfast and again at tea-time!

The ironic part of the whole business was that what went up had to come down. The drains in the pig pens led simply to their doors, so what Kropje termed 'ze liquid man-you-are' just gravitated back down the yard towards the house. Before the winter was half run the entire yard was awash with pig muck, my friend the midden having joined forces to spread in all directions. Nothing we did by way of restraining it was effective for long and eventually the thick black carpet spread past the front door itself to the very gate. Visitors, such as the postman, were hard put to it to reach the house dry-shod, and then only by skirting round the edges. We made innumerable attempts to stem the flow by sweeping and taking out of barrowloads, but it was a losing battle, aided and abetted as it was by the unusually mild and wet winter.

It was at this juncture that we received a visit from our old 'friend' Mr Morgan, the milk production officer from the Ministry, who had left us in peace for almost a year. Unfortunately for me, Bill had gone off to town that day, so I paddled out to see him.

'What on earth's happened here then, boyo?' he started in an unpleasant tone, evidently somewhat awestruck by the sea of muck where none had been before.

'Er … whey, don't you know? It … er … tends to undermine the muck heap.'

'Well, you can tell your brother from me,' he barked in measured tones, 'that I want this yard cleaned all the way from by here to the front gate. You understand?'

'Yes, right ho. I'll pass it on.'

'I'll be round again before Lady Day, and it will need to be perfect by then, or else!' he added, threateningly, before driving off.

When Bill got back and heard what Morgan had said, he looked distinctly worried, for his milk producer's licence meant everything to him, and it was clearly in jeopardy as things stood.

'He's absolutely right, of course,' he admitted. 'One of the standard regulations is that there shall be no manure within twenty-five yards of the cowshed or dairy. It's a wonder he wasn't nastier about it, really.'

'Well, we'll just have to drop everything and get busy with the wheelbarrow again,' I sighed. 'I expect Gareth will give a hand with his horse and cart if he knows it's desperate.'

'What we need is a tractor and trailer, and the sooner the better,' Bill snorted. 'I'm going to give up waiting for Watkyn and start going to all the farm sales I can. Let's have another look at the paper.'

And so, urged on by the desperate state of the yard, Bill started going off in the taxi to all farm sales within range, while I was left holding the fort. On one of these occasions an extremely Welsh AI man came to inseminate one of the cows and I took him into the cowshed, a job always done previously by Bill.

'Yammak?' inquired the AI man, getting out his instruments.

'What was that?' I hesitated, trying to look intelligent.

'Yammak?' he repeated, rather forcibly.

'I didn't quite catch,' I said, after straining my brain to interpret the word.

'YAMMAK!' he bawled, despairingly, as he seized the cow's ear to find its earmark and gave me up for a nut case.

'Oh, I see … I'm sorry… Yes, of course, silly of me,' I muttered, not wanting to endanger proceedings by alluding to his odd pronunciation.

Another day, a travelling Sikh salesman arrived at the door with a huge suitcase, just after I'd started to fry myself a few rashers of bacon for lunch. I was so sorry for him having to hump such a weight around that I determined to buy something if at all possible but, despite his lengthy extolling of the virtues of each item he produced from the bottomless case, I continued to hesitate. At long last we came to some ties and I settled for one of those before returning to my lunch preparations. To my astonishment there was no sign of the bacon rashers I'd left on a low gas, and at first I suspected friend Trigger, but eventually I realised that they had been completely rendered down in the hot fat, a fact of life I would not have credited before that day. I decided against bacon for lunch and settled for some cheese instead.

It must have been about the fifth spring sale Bill went to that brought success. When the old taxi hadn't returned by six o'clock I guessed he must have found something at last, and waited expectantly as darkness fell. Long before I heard anything, Trigger began to 'woof' with his ears cocked towards the gate and out we went together to welcome what I hoped would be a nice little tractor and trailer suitable for our dangerous slopes.

Leaning on the gate with Trigger on a leash and an oil pressure lamp balanced on the bank, I soon detected the approach of something way up the lane. The sound was a mixture of clanking and gravel grinding and, did I imagine it, or were those sparks flying up over the hedge as the thing approached?

'Great grief! Has he gone and bought a steam-roller, Trigger?' I gasped, as I distinctly heard a chuffing sound above the general racket in the lane.

The vehicle, whatever it was, had no lights but at least it wasn't a steam-roller, I saw, as it came clanking round the final bend. Steel front wheels and a chimney spouting sparks certainly, but it was a tractor of sorts, and as Bill drove triumphantly into the light of the pressure lamp, laughing his head off on his high perch, I got a clear view of a huge steam traction-engine, complete with spinning flywheel and towing an outsize two-wheeled trailer behind!

Vendre Fach had entered the Age of Steam!

Chapter 22

Into the Steam Age

'It was just too good a bargain to miss,' explained Bill when I had recovered my wind from laughing at his hilarious purchase. 'They opened the bidding at a hundred pounds, but there weren't any takers even when he dropped to seventy-five, so it was withdrawn. Neither of the tractors went cheaply, so I found the owner afterwards and offered him fifty for it. He agreed on condition I took the trailer as well, which was also unsold, for another fifteen. So there we are – quite a bargain, I reckon!'

'And how come it's still in working order? It must be a hundred years old, surely?'

'A hundred years my foot! The date is shown on that brass plate there. 1926, isn't it?'

I peered at the plate Bill indicated, straining my eyes in the poor light to decipher it. 'Ah, yes. Suppliers ... Caractacus or someone, Flint, 1926. Hmm ... well, I'm blowed!

Who'd have thought it?'

'Not Caractacus, surely? – Caradoc Bros.,' said Bill, bringing over the lamp to prove his point.

'Well, it looks like something they used to fight the Romans with. Caractacus would be about right for vintage, I'd say!'

'Apparently she was used for general work on the farm right up till the end of the war, and since then she has been driving a dynamo as a stationary engine,' Bill went on. 'They converted her to oil as soon as the wartime shortages ended.'

The trailer, so far from being a nice handy size for our steep fields, resembled nothing so much as an Army tank transporter, solid metal throughout apart from its huge tyres slung amidships.

'We'll soon shift the muck with that baby!' enthused Bill. 'The farmer told me it'll take five tons easily.'

'Just as well it's got a powerful horse to hold it,' I remarked. 'I wouldn't fancy that loaded up behind something like a Fergy!'

That evening, Bill and I were like children who keep returning to their new toys on Christmas Day to make sure they are not a dream. Each time we crossed the yard we would feast our eyes on the smoking monster standing quietly in the shadows, with its shining brass appendages and impressive chimney stack, and we could talk of little else for days.

Caractacus, as we naturally came to call the old traction engine, made a big hit with the neighbours, too. As soon as it had got up steam next morning, a slight hiccup which meant a lengthy delay before the old thing could move, it chuffed across the fields to be introduced to Eirwen and Gareth.

Gales of laughter floating from the Bryn-coed direction told me it was going down well, and before long the old engine came chugging back on to the Vendre yard with all three in the cockpit and Eirwen, beside herself with excitement, at the wheel. Evans-the-Road was put in mind of several gripping anecdotes we hadn't heard before, while Kropje clearly viewed the huge ensemble with mixed feelings but somehow refrained from saying 'Veel do'. The only derogatory note was struck by Charlie who stared at it for several minutes before announcing that he wouldn't risk his neck on a thing like that, whatever.

We wasted no time in getting stuck into the job-to-end-jobs, clearing the yard of its much carpet all the way from 'by here' to 'by there', as Morgan had decreed. Fortunately, perhaps, we were unable to achieve anything like the size of load the trailer was built for, on account of the unstable nature of the commodity being handled. Indeed, the technique we were forced to employ was to build first a little bank of passably solid material around the trailer's edges, and then to scoop in shovelfuls of the nasty black slurry to fill up the middle. Once a depth of a few inches was achieved, at the cost of many a foul smelling splash in the face, Bill would ease the sloppy load out along the lane to the three-cornered field with as little loss by spillage en route as careful driving could achieve. Even so, the lane did suffer its quota and by no means all that set out reached its destination in the field.

Notwithstanding the capacity of the trailer, it took us at least a week to complete that particular Labour of Hercules, sweeping every vestige of slurry as we went, to reveal once more the gravelly surface of the original yard. Towards the end, the muck became more manageable and we were able to increase the size of each load in consequence. Bill also became more playful with his outsize toy as he grew accustomed to it, and started trying it out for speed and manoeuvrability. But the job got done, the yard regained its pristine purity and we chalked up the first of many great achievements to our new iron horse. Morgan was welcome now, whenever he liked; we no longer lived under the cloud of his impending visit.

'I hope old Caractacus is safe,' I remarked to Bill one evening. 'I mean, it hasn't been moved for years, apparently, and now you're chucking it about like a bren-gun carrier on Salisbury Plain!'

'Good Lord, of course it's safe,' retorted Bill, impatiently. 'Everything's made of cast iron, strong enough to haul a train.'

'Even so, it might be an idea to get Watkyn to give it the once-over, don't you think?'

'Go on with you – don't be an old woman! I've had a good look underneath. The steering linkage is a hundred per cent, there are no tyres to worry about and the engine is its own brake. What more could we want?'

'Oh, well, you're the driver!' I said, dropping the subject.

Once the yard-cleaning job was out of the way, Bill started putting his new baby to all sorts of hair-raising tests. First we spent a couple of days pulling out old tree-stumps, a spectacular and satisfying game spiced with the ever-present chance of a snapping chain around one's ears. There were quite a few such stumps about the farm, sawn off as low as possible but with substantial roots spreading in all directions, and Caractacus made an impressive sight as he flexed his iron muscles with much puffing and blowing, prior to tearing out the stumps, roots and all. When there were no more stumps to pull we chuffed off up to the woods to collect a load of timber we'd cut but failed to carry when the autumn had turned prematurely wet. Turning the massive combination, in the confined and sloping space, gave me another crop of grey hairs as Bill seemed determined to find out just how far he could lean it over before it toppled, rather like those double-decker bus tests of stability where the vehicle somehow stays on its wheels despite the crazy angles to which it is pressed.

But the real trial of Providence came when Bill decided to descend the near-vertical field below the house to bring up the roots we'd stored in a clamp at the bottom. 'It's too damned steep!' I protested. 'The old tractor wasn't built for mountaineering – it'll tip over!' but I might as well have saved my breath; Bill was looking forward to some more fun, and that was an end to the matter. So down the steep ramp we went, with its sheer edge on the lower side, turning abruptly nose downward on reaching the field so as to counter the perils of the slope, while I balanced as best I could on the trailer. The bottom was reached without mishap and we loaded up the bulk of the Swedes and mangolds remaining after the winter feeding, till the front of the trailer would take no more.

'We need all the weight we can get on the front so as to give the wheels a good grip,' explained Bill, as we prepared to climb back up to the lane above us. 'Now for it!'

With a flurry of black smoke, as he took the strain, the snorting Caractacus headed directly for the steepest section, while I trudged alongside, keeping my fingers firmly crossed. All seemed to be going well and I was beginning to think perhaps I was imagining the dangers when I suddenly noticed the front wheels had ceased to turn. They were floating over the ground with just a delicate touch here and there on the rougher bits.

'STOP, STOP!' I yelled with panic gestures. 'THE FRONT WHEELS!'

'I can't stop or we'll never make it!'

shouted Bill, peering down at the wheels from his high perch. 'Jump on the front, quick!'

Risking my all, I managed to scramble in front of the rearing monster, get my feet on the front axle and cling precariously to the hot front plate as we surged on up the slope. My weight seemed to tip the scales, for the wheels kept turning now, but my pulse was going through the sound barrier when we levelled out at the top and I felt as if I'd aged ten years in about three minutes.

'I told you it was too damned steep!' I gasped, as Bill stopped to let me get off. 'The bloody thing was about to go over backwards!'

'Oh, I don't expect so,' grinned Bill, obviously finding it all rather exhilarating. 'They go so far and then reach a sort of equilibrium. She'd probably have got up O.K., but it was the steering I was worried about.'

'Well, you needn't think I'm doing that little act again!' I retorted hotly. 'What would have happened if I'd slipped off? It would have been curtains, that's what!' For once in a while I was not amused; indeed I was shaking like a leaf.

The following day being a Sunday, I adjourned to the house as soon as the routine jobs were completed after breakfast, to go through the weekly ritual of straightening the place up and preparing the Sunday lunch. We tried to avoid any extra jobs outside on this one day of the week, and Bill would usually follow me indoors around noon to light the kitchen fire so that we could have a bit of a sit-down with the papers after lunch. While I was deeply immersed in washing up the mountain of dirty crocks and cutlery, I heard Caractacus approach and chuff along towards the gate.

'Now, what on earth's he up to?' I mused. 'Holy smoke! He's going down to get the rest of the roots, I do believe!'

From my vantage point at the sink I saw him negotiate the steep ramp easily enough, and turn down towards the clamp at the bottom. It all looked so easy that I began to wonder if maybe I was a bit of an old woman after all.

I knew there was only a small load remaining, and I reasoned that the weight on the drawbar would be appreciably less than last time, so that the front wheels would be unlikely to lift as they had done then. With this reassuring thought I turned my attention back to my chores, completed the

186

washing-up, resurrected the tablecloth and pitched into the potatoes.

Bill seemed to be taking his time and I was beginning to wonder if I would have to make the gravy when the door opened and in he walked, looking a bit sheepish.

'What's happened to Caractacus?' I started, looking up.

'Nothing very much,' returned Bill. 'A wheel's come off, that's all!'

Chapter 23

Digging the Silage Pit

As soon as I'd recovered a little from the shock news about Caractacus's wheel, I left Bill to get on with lighting the fire and popped out to view the sad scene from the lane. There was the old engine near the bottom of the steep field, all down on one knee and looking very dejected indeed. Bill had just swung it round on leaving the clamp with the loaded trailer, so that he was heading directly up the slope when disaster struck. The nearside front wheel was lying alongside the crippled tractor, but Bill reckoned it had simply worked loose as there was no sign of anything shorn off. With any luck it would just have to be put back on, but that was obviously a job for Watkyn and his heavy tackle. I couldn't help wondering what would have happened if the wheel had come off during one of Bill's wilder gyrations, or while negotiating the ramp. I shuddered to think of it.

When I arrived at Watkyn's place later that day to tell him the news, he was sitting in front of the 'telly' – he was the first in the village to get one – watching some trashy play with his cap on. I'd noticed on a previous visit that his taste in literature was a bit basic – boys' comics to be exact – and now I was to get a sample of what he watched on the box, something obviously meant for ten-year-olds but with plenty of action.

'COME IN, BOY!' he shouted when, in desperation, I poked my head round the door. 'Take a seat for a minute.'

I didn't much care for his habit of calling me 'boy' in my late twenties, nor did I enjoy having to await his pleasure while he sat transfixed with his back to me. But, resisting the impulse to stride over and interrupt the play, which would never have done as we were so dependent on his goodwill, I sat and suffered for about twenty minutes before it finished and he deigned to turn his attention in my direction.

'Lost a wheel then, is it, boy?' he remarked when I had explained. 'Well, I've got a funeral on tomorrow, but I'll be up with you as soon as I get back. How's that?'

'Very kind of you, Watkyn, but remember it's pretty solid and you'll probably need a crane to lift it.'

I wish I'd been present to see his reactions when he arrived the following afternoon, for he hadn't seen Caractacus before and he had a most expressive, not to say comical, face. But, by the time I got back from a visit to the shop, he and Bill had got the wheel on again with the aid of several planks and an outsize jack.

'I don't think you'll 'ave no more trouble with this one, leastways,' grunted the tough little Watkyn, heaving on a huge spanner to tighten the big end-nut, 'but I'll check the other one while I'm at it.' He didn't seem in the least concerned that such a thing had happened, but clearly shared Bill's view that it was all a little joke. The fact that someone might have been killed didn't enter into it.

'What about the rest of it, Watkyn?' I

managed to get in while Bill was out of earshot. 'D'you think it's safe?'

'Aye! Safe as 'ouses, mun, as long as you don't try nothing too fancy, whatever. Mind you,' he added, kneeling underneath the boiler and peering up at the back wheels, 'them buggers look like they was put there by moonlight! But I expect they'll 'old.'

With this disturbing observation from the expert, we adjourned to the house for a beer, while Caractacus was left to get some steam going. It was a relief to know there was nothing broken, though, as we realised spare parts for the old tractor were going to be out of the question, and we would have to rely on the ingenuity of Watkyn to keep it on the road at all.

'Well, how did the funeral go, Watkyn?' asked Bill, cheerfully, as we sank our drinks in the kitchen.

'Oh, lovely! Crowds of people there, too. It was a "bring-your-knife" you see; much the best way, indeed.'

'It was a what, did you say?'

'A "bring-your-knife" we do call it. All the women guests brings their knives to 'elp with the sandwiches. Yes, a lovely funeral,' he added wistfully.

Not long after the drama of Caractacus's losing a wheel, the pompous Mr Morgan put in his expected appearance to check on the state of the yard. From what I could catch of the conversation from one of the out-buildings, Bill was doing his best to insinuate that Morgan had dreamt the whole business of a muck crisis while, for his part, Morgan was condescending to let the matter pass now that things had been so thoroughly restored to normal. It was just as well the yard had been cleaned, it struck me, or the highly polished riding boots that Morgan was sporting that day might have lost some of their shine, but Bill soon took him off to the rough field below the barn to ask his advice on siting our silage pit, the next major job on the agenda now that the ground was drying out and spring was in the air.

I got on with my job of sorting seed potatoes in one of the barns until I heard Morgan's car start up and drive away, when I wandered down to hear the upshot re the silage pit. Bill had disappeared but, sticking my head through the back door in search of him, I was surprised to see him feeding titbits to Trigger, supported by much affectionate patting.

'What did he do?' I queried. 'Bite Morgan

or something?'

'Better than that – he lifted his leg against his smart riding boots!'

Bill took me out to see where the pit was going to be. They had decided it should be dug as close as possible to the hedge skirting the lane, so as to facilitate carting the stuff when the time came, but it would have to be driven into the slope of the field, at right angles to the hedge, so as to help its natural drainage.

'And how big has it got to be?' I queried, apprehensively.

'Sixteen feet by nine, he recommends, with an average depth of about four feet. But into that slope it will be about six feet deep at the top end.'

'Well, let's hope it's soft going, that's all!' I sighed.

Soon after Morgan's visit we equipped ourselves with a spade, a pickaxe, an iron crowbar and a couple of shovels and started on the pit which was to put all other jobs we ever attempted in the shade. We began happily enough, cutting the rough turf into rectangles and stacking them neatly round the measured edges but, even if the going had remained good throughout we should have faced a formidable task in removing some six hundred or so cubic feet of earth and ejecting it by shovel power. As it was, we struck rock or, more exactly, shale at about eighteen inches, which recurred in ever more concentrated patches all the way down. Some measure of the effort that went into it can be gleaned from the fact that the heavy crowbar, which was called upon times without number for breaking through the shale, sustained a distinct bend in the course of proceedings, and the other implements were never to be the same again. The last straw, to my mind, was the massive mound of soil which accumulated round the edges of the pit. Try as we would, it always encroached with the result that our shovelfuls had to be flung, in the later stages, not just six or seven feet above the level of the working, but more like nine or ten. There was no question of abandoning the site and trying elsewhere, for the likelihood was that the entire field was shale-ridden, perhaps even the whole farm; so we struggled on, and I began to fear we'd never reach the depth we needed. We must have spent just about the entire month of April slogging in that pit before Bill finally agreed to call it a day, and I vowed I would never dig another silage pit as long as I lived.

'Why the hell hasn't anyone invented a machine to do this job?' I gasped, exhausted, as we surveyed the finished article.

'Oh, they have!' replied Bill, cheerfully. 'It's a box-like contraption that fits on to the front of a tractor. Most people hire a contractor with one, but there's no sense in throwing money away, is there?'

We were determined to get a siderake, the revolving hay machine which would both turn the swaths and rake them into rows for making into haycocks or for baling. Seeing one advertised in a farm 'clear-out' sale, Bill decided to go after it and, never having been to one of these affairs before, I went along to sample the fun.

There is a real sense of excitement at these sales, where genuine bargains are often to be had since it is in everyone's interest to get rid of the stuff, and they make a day out for the farmers, so many of whom are known to one another. In those parts most of the talk was in Welsh, though the actual auctions were conducted in English, no doubt for the likes of Bill and myself.

The countryside always seems to breed a greater diversity of human types than the town, and I found myself rubbing shoulders with some very odd specimens, not a few of them uncouth to a degree. I always felt a bit like Bob Hope, in that sort of company, when he shuffled into a cowboy saloon bar and, in an effort to impress the thugs lounging about, asked for a Scotch 'in a dirty glass'. I had the same trouble in trying to blend with the surroundings and in endeavouring to adapt my lily-white English voice to the rough accents of the clientele. Sissy-looking Englishmen were not appreciated in that company, but Bill always managed to command respect, probably on account of his towering physique.

For all that, there was a lot going on to interest and entertain us as we waited till well into the afternoon for the siderake to come up. The auctioneers in action are worth going a long way to hear as they mingle witticisms in English and Welsh with their quick-fire patter and, for all their rough appearance, the farmers are full of humour, though much of it in Welsh and so, unfortunately, going over our heads.

Bill made no mistake in nodding through his bids when the time came and, after giving instructions to a one-eared gentleman haulier, we set off back for home in the Old Girl, looking forward to a reviving cup of tea before starting to catch up on the routine work.

But there was a shock in store for, on entering the Vendre kitchen, we found such a scene of desolation as only a tornado could have been expected to achieve. Somehow we'd failed to shut the back door properly before leaving, the hens had found it open, hopped up on the crumb-covered table and set about it with a vengeance. Crockery was lying broken in all directions, the tablecloth was in shreds from their sharp claws, our precious butter – still rationed – had disappeared with most of its wrapping, and there was chicken muck everywhere. The fifty hens had had a field day.

Chapter 24

The Milestone of Mechanised Milking

As spring once again brought its magic touch to the fields and hedgerows several of our young stock calved down, to boost the milk yield well above anything we had achieved to date. The combination of the 'Spring Flush', as the sudden annual surge in milk yield, resulting from the new grass, is known, together with the calving down of some half-dozen heifers, brought the number of churns up to five for the first time. It also made the job of milking so much bigger that we began to think seriously of installing a milking machine, the idea being to use Caractacus's great flywheel as the power unit and so avoid the need to purchase a petrol engine to drive the vacuum pump.

When Bill broached the subject with Watkyn, the response was that he had nothing suitable in stock but thought he could get hold of one capable of being driven by Caractacus in a matter of weeks. In the meantime he wondered if we'd like to use a funny little Japanese milking machine he had taken recently in part exchange. This was a remarkably compact little device, incorporating petrol engine and vacuum pump in a portable unit which could be set up behind each cow in turn. Bill had never seen one of these little machines before and was a bit sceptical about its abilities, but so anxious were we for some relief in the cowshed that he grabbed at the chance and Watkyn duly brought it up one sunny afternoon.

Although Bill was concerned about how

the cows would react to a noisy engine just behind them, after being accustomed to the peace and tranquillity of hand-milking, it seemed to me that my prayers had at long last been answered. Here was the succour my soul had cried out for during all those hours of discomfort and effort on the three-legged stool, and I could hardly bring myself to believe that the purgatory was really at an end. For, of all the killing jobs the farm had produced, hand-milking won the accolade in my book, a twice daily wrestling match that I never really got the hang of.

There was certainly a frightful clatter in the cowshed when we came to use the little machine for the first time that evening. Even so, the older cows, most of which had been machine-milked in their time, took to it fairly well, even old Jane, who called for almost superhuman squeeze power by hand, milking out quite rapidly. It was a different story with the younger cows, but Bill's experienced handling of them brought us through without any major mishaps and it looked as though the tiny machine was going to prove an unqualified success.

'I think they'll get used to it all right in a few days,' puffed Bill. 'But now for old Bastard-Features – she's sure to object!' We had left my friend Minnie till last, knowing her propensities for trouble, and now we stationed the rattling engine a yard or two behind her, gave her an outsize ration of her favourite cow-cake, and applied the cluster of teat-cups. She disapproved from the start and was soon describing elegant arcs with her back legs in an effort to put the kybosh on proceedings. Bill performed prodigies of agility in restraining the cluster from falling off while I took up my familiar station at the front end, bending her leg at the 'knee' and straining to support her entire weight as she mixed her battle tactics, occasionally going right down to improve her range. When hostilities were at their height, one of Minnie's backward high kicks scored a direct hit on the poor little engine, knocking it on its back, pulling off the cluster and stopping the motor in one fell stroke.

My friend was looking pretty wild-eyed by this time, but seemed to calm down visibly as we heaved without success on the starter cord. Try as we would the thing refused so much as to fire again and we were obliged to give it up in disgust, Bill setting off with it there and then up to Watkyn's in the hope that he could put it right for the morning milking.

When he got back about an hour later, I was shattered to learn that Minnie's remarkable coup de pied had bent the main shaft of the little engine and the thing was now quite useless. So much for our having reached the milestone of mechanised milking. We were now back to square one and we crawled off to bed in a state of some dejection.

During the ensuing three weeks or so of continuing hard labour on the milking stool, while waiting for Watkyn to get us a proper machine, I had to agree with Bill that perhaps Minnie was something less than perfect after all. But eventually the new system was all set up, with Caractacus driving a belt through the end wall of the cowshed, a vacuum pipe running along behind the cows and two shining new buckets complete with clusters. The whole apparatus set us back the best part of a hundred pounds, but it seemed to me the finest investment we'd ever made and it wasn't long before the cows grew accustomed to the noise, even Minnie suffering it better than hand-milking as time went on. The only factor on the debit side was the additional washing-up but, whatever way we looked at it, we had taken a major stride.

One of the heifers that calved down that spring was none other than Bill's protégée and pride, Bridget, our first and most promising calf, of whom we expected great things. Rather like a beautiful child, she had been admired by everyone who ever saw her, combining as she did the looks and the pedigree of a real winner. It was, therefore, with considerable concern that Bill noticed a certain hardness in her udder on first stripping her out just prior to calving and he wasted no time in sending for Lewis the vet, not wanting to take any risks with this of all our animals.

'She's got a serious infection,' announced Lewis after inspecting her. 'It's what we call Summer Mastitis – not mastitis at all, really. We'll be lucky if we can save that quarter. You must milk it out every three hours and I'll call again tomorrow dinner-time to see how she is.'

This was a blow, indeed. Nobody could have carried out the instructions more con-scientiously than Bill did – he was up half the night – but long before Lewis's scheduled call the following day, he was getting nothing out of an increasingly swollen quarter.

'I don't like the look of it, but I'll have another go,' said Lewis when he arrived.

After some time spent probing with his instruments he had freed the blocked duct, and our instructions were to continue with the three-hourly stripping for a further twenty-four hours. 'Ring me in the morning if it's blocked again,' said Lewis as he took his leave.

Having a sick cow is a bit like illness in the house; it weighs heavily on all you do and takes away the joy of living. This was our first real experience of this unpleasant aspect of animal husbandry and we could do nothing but carry out our instructions and hope for the best. But we were worried sick, and after another awful night Bill went off to the village to 'phone the news that the quarter was again blocked solid.

'I suppose she'll just lose the quarter,' explained Bill, 'though I believe there's a danger of losing the cow with this particular germ. Anyhow, Lewis said he'll be out directly, so we'll just have to await his verdict.'

So we waited, apprehensively, for Lewis to come. We didn't have to wait long, fortunately, but neither of us was prepared for the dramatic Welsh touch he brought to the business. Leaping from his car while it still seemed to be moving, he brandished an already opened cut-throat razor at arm's length and made straight for the cowshed without a word. With a deft flick of the razor he sliced through the offending teat before poor Bridget knew he was there. A disgusting splatter of clotted milk and blood sprayed the floor while Bill and I looked on aghast.

'No use messin' about,' said Lewis. 'She'll just have to be a three quarter cow, that's all!'

'Yes,' gulped Bill, for once looking a bit shaken.

'Hot water, soap and towel,' barked Lewis, giving me my chance to leave the painful scene.

That spring we grazed the grass by electric fencer, a tremendous advance on the ordinary method of turning the herd into a field to graze haphazardly. With the fencer it is possible to give the cows a yard or two's width of entirely untouched grass to graze, stretching the length of the field, moving the fence a yard or so daily until the growth is all consumed. This is very much more efficient use of resources than is the extensive grazing technique where so many large patches of grass remain uneaten through having been mucked upon or trodden down. I was intrigued to see how soon cows learn to avoid touching the wire, and how they will often stretch their necks beneath it to get the limit of their ration. It was amusing, too, to see the younger and brasher members of the herd recoil a time or two and thereafter treat the flimsy wire with marked respect. Not so amusing, on the other hand, when one inadvertently touched the wire oneself, as was inevitable from time to time.

The shock coming off a six-volt battery, as it does, is supposed to be quite harmless, but it is a nasty jolt for all that, and we had many a laugh at one another getting caught at various times, one of the best, to my mind, being when Bill slipped jumping over it in his hobnailed boots, only to have the wire catch in a stud.

Bill's own idea of a joke was to switch on playfully while I was adjusting the far end of the fence, perhaps up against the distant hedge, but his crowning achievement was in 'catching' Kropje one afternoon. Not only did the Latvian claim to be unaffected by the shock but he had a maddening habit of ducking under the wire, thereby dislodging a post or two, instead of hopping over as everyone else did. To counter this tendency

Bill deliberately sank the posts in a few inches deeper than usual, knowing that Kropje was coming over to walk that way. When the old boy attempted his duck-under technique he got about half-way before recoiling like a shot from a gun. The low wire had touched the nape of his neck.

Chapter 25

'Plenty of Money With Me!'

During the early part of that second full summer at Vendre we were honoured by a visit from our stunning young sister, Heather. Whether she came to escape for a bit from her many admirers or to sample the rural life, we weren't too sure, but we were delighted to have her as much for her lively company as for the badly needed touch of comfort she brought to our bachelor home. We turned the little parlour into a bedroom and made her as comfortable as the lack of mod cons would permit. I think she found it all rather idyllic, as indeed it was in summer, and her planned fortnight's stay lengthened into about six weeks.

Some of our little ways, however, evolved over almost two years of basic living, came in for Heather's disapproval. She drew the line at dung-covered boots being worn at meals, refusing to eat with us unless we changed into slippers; she took exception to our throwing tea-cup slops into the sink from where we sat at table; she insisted on buying a cloth for washing-up purposes instead of using our hands for the job as was our wont; and she declared unhygienic our habit of keeping the weekly joint, in hot weather, from the Friday when it arrived till the Sunday morning, simply washing it down in vinegar to counter the smelliness before cooking.

It was in her determination to pre-cook the joint on arrival, indeed, that Heather met her first Vendre crisis, for while she was wrestling with the adjustments of the infuriating oil stove burners, Trigger calmly filched the juicy wing-rib from the table behind her and made off with it through the open door. Eventually succeeding in getting the required blue flames, Heather turned to take up the meat, quickly guessed what had happened and dashed out in search of Trigger. By the time she had tracked him down, nestling under the hayrick, and snatched back our week's meat supply from beneath his paws, the joint was looking decidedly torn and ragged. So she decided, after all, to resort to the vinegar treatment, sluicing down thoroughly and trimming off the more tatty edges before pushing it into the oven according to plan. Very sensibly she mentioned nothing of all this to her squeamish brothers till weeks later, so we were able to relish the meal as we did all Heather's cooking.

Nor did our pretty sister limit her activities to the domestic front. She came with me over the mountains on a pilgrimage to the boar, threw the sops through the little window when things looked threatening, and joined in the pig pantomime with the cultured Mr Rhys when we got there. She drove the Old Girl round the hayfields for Bill and me to load when we weren't using Caractacus for one reason or another, and she took over the feeding of the numerous baby calves we had recently acquired. She even went with Bill in the taxi one Wednesday to sample the rough company of the livestock mart.

It happened that Kropje, too, wanted a lift to market that day but, with Heather occupying the luggage space alongside Bill, he was obliged to travel in the back with the week-old bull calf being taken in for sale. Like most farmers Kropje managed to transform his appearance for visits to town, and Heather was surprised to see him looking very respectable in a smart sports jacket and cavalry twill trousers.

Just as they were passing through the village of Pen-y-bont Fawr, however, loud shouts and banging from the rear prompted Bill to draw in to the side. Out clambered Kropje with a sickly smile and the announcement that he had decided to change his mode of conveyance.

'You haf feeded ze calf too vell!' he explained, showing a badly soiled sleeve and trousers as evidence. 'I veel take ze 'bus from here!'

While at the market Bill bought another Wessex saddleback sow and litter to add to our porker enterprise which was proving a success. Heather was quite fascinated, as well she might have been, by the auction and the clientele thereof, a more uncouth-looking set of ruffians being hard to imagine. The farmers themselves, I always feel, are a rugged bunch, but the hangers-on at livestock marts are enough to make the flesh creep. I imagine many of them fall into the category of 'farm boys', a Welsh euphemism for country simpletons who live on the farms and do a lot of the rough work in return for their keep. These visits to market are probably their only contact with the outside world and, in consequence, they tend to lack the social graces. There is also a fair sprinkling of near-morons employed at the mart itself, pushing animals into the auction ring and generally helping the auctioneers. Not that the dealers and butchers can claim to add much tone to the gathering, with many lacking fingers and even ears, as if they occasionally let fly at one another with their cleavers. But probably the thing which serves most to make these marts depressing is the plight of the animals themselves. Completely bewildered, they are pushed and pummelled, usually with sticks, from one pen to another, into the ring and round it, into lorries and out of them and for many it is their last hour. The whole business is grim to a degree, with its soulless operators and butchers leering on the sidelines, and it always upset me to go at all. No wonder Heather was shocked – most sensitive people would be – but as Bill explained afterwards in an attempt to pacify her, something of the sort has to take place as long as mankind continues to eat meat. And despite appearances, the marts were, in fact, very strictly controlled, with RSPCA officials constantly in attendance. To some extent Heather's indignation was offset by the comical little saddleback piglets they brought back, with their mother, in the taxi. Like me she had never seen tiny piglets before and their antics held her spellbound.

One sunny afternoon, a week or so after she came to stay, Heather decided to take Trigger for a walk along the river bank. It proved a pleasant ramble but rather hard going, with overgrown hedges and brambles to negotiate, so that when she eventually came out on the road somewhere between Tresiliog and the farm, she decided to stick to it rather than return the way she had come. She hadn't been walking on the road long, however, before she heard a car approaching behind her and, having succeeded in grabbing Trigger, she looked up to see Watkyn's comical son, Emrys, at the wheel of their ancient hearse. Although she had no real wish for a lift she accepted Emrys's offer and was soon bowling along in the huge old Rolls. It was a new experience to ride in a hearse and Heather was as tickled to draw up in it at the farm as Bill and I were to see her arrive. What with rides in the old taxi, on the footplate of Caractacus and now in a hearse, her motoring experience was taking some interesting turns, and she thought the lift a great joke, giving Emrys a dazzling smile as she alighted with Trigger on the yard.

She wasn't quite so amused, though, when the following Sunday evening Emrys reappeared all togged up in a smart new cap and oil-free clothes. He made no direct reference to the purpose of his call and Bill and I were a bit slow in putting two and two together, probably because Emrys was, to say the least, somewhat untypical of Heather's beaux. Not only was he a real country yokel with everything short of the piece of straw in his mouth, but he was twice her age if he was a day. We asked him in for a beer and he stayed for an hour, keeping his cap on throughout, even when sitting in an armchair in front of our Sunday fire. After each of his many anecdotes he would add casually, 'Plenty of money with me, you see!' by way, we imagined, of softening up the defences.

When Heather related these events to Mrs Lloyd-Vaughan she hooted with mirth. 'You poor dear! Emrys of all people! You see, the custom in these parts is for the man to call three Sundays running to show he's in earnest. So, whatever you do, you mustn't be at home the next two Sunday evenings. You're to come here to tea and I'll run you home at bedtime.'

Sure enough, Emrys turned up again on the following two Sundays. It was a bit awkward explaining to him that Heather was out but he put a brave face on it, stayed just as long, kept his cap on as before, slipped in the 'Plenty of money with me' ploy several more times, and made no direct reference to Heather at all. But he must have got the message, poor chap, as he never came again after his three-week stint was done.

As for Heather, she still ranks Emrys as the least promising of her many suitors, even though she looks back on her ride in the hearse with some nostalgia.

Chapter 26

John and Davey 'Clydach'

Heather and I were chatting over a protracted cup of coffee after lunch one day, Bill having taken himself back to his job in the field with his customary self-discipline when, unbeknown to anyone, Elsie the sow decided to emerge from her sty to see what the world had to offer. Throwing away her door like a toffee paper, she proceeded to waddle around the yard in search of something edible, and eventually finding a door unlatched she started, in her cautious way, to nose in. Exactly what it was that frightened her we never discovered but, having got her head and shoulders through the door, she decided to withdraw again, only to find herself effectively jammed by the heavy door, hung on self-closing hinges as it was. The harder she pulled backwards the tighter the door gripped against her great ears and, at this stage, she started to emit terrifying screams.

I was on the scene in no time and laid about her rear end with a convenient muck-fork in an effort to persuade the huge animal to go forward rather than back, but to little avail. The situation was looking pretty desperate when 'LOOK OUT!' came Bill's voice above the din. I glanced up just in time to see him charging up the yard and flinging himself, shoulder first, at Elsie's posterior. In a trice the sow shot forward, it was all over and we were having our usual laugh together, with Heather almost in hysterics. Not for the first time I was glad to have Bill around when an animal got into trouble.

The second of the local beaux to make a pass at Heather was none other than Eirwen's eighty-five-year-old grandfather, a delightful old boy who was often at Brycoed during the summer months. Old 'Dang-It', as we knew him by virtue of his frequent use of that expression, often called at Vendre on his walks, but Maida Granitt didn't share our approval of him. ''E's a dirty old man, that one!' she told Heather soon after her arrival. Bill and I found this rather hard to swallow but had to admit he went a bit far in trying to put his arm round Heather the first time they met. So the next time we saw him approaching across the fields she and Maida adjourned to the hay barn to hide on top of the rick till he'd gone.

The poor old chap spent his usual ten minutes passing the time of day in farm chat before mooching off in the direction of some other neighbour, whereupon I went to get the women back in circulation. By way of getting a laugh I tried to imitate Dang-It's gruff voice as I approached the bottom of the rick.

'Dang it!' I croaked. 'I wonder where they are? They must be about 'ere somewhere. Dang it! Up on the rick I shouldn't wonder!' As I started to climb the ladder I exaggerated the 'dang its' to the point of idiocy.

'Dang it! Where are they? Dang it! They're hiding from me I'm sure! Dang it! Dang it! Dang it!' I rambled on, making the joke as absurd as I could so as to obviate any chance of their being taken in. But when I reached the topmost rungs and peered over the edge of the hay I was amazed to see Maida Granitt glaring in my direction with an 'over-my-dead-body' expression. Somewhere behind her lay Heather trying to melt into the hayrick.

For a long moment Maida stared at me, seemingly uncomprehending. Then, 'It's your brother!' she gasped, in a stunned voice.

'What?' squeaked a most un-typical Heather from the background.

'It's your brother!'

'My brother?'

'Yes, it's all right, it's only your brother!'

It seemed to take several minutes for the truth to register, and it was obvious that they had been completely taken in. I could feel them trembling as I helped them down the ladder amidst protestations of innocent intentions on my part. But Trigger wasn't the only one in the doghouse that evening.

Although the comical Emrys and the octogenarian 'Dang-It' failed to make a favourable impression, the brothers John and Davey 'Clydach' did make something of a conquest, if not in quite the same direction. Davey was in the shop one afternoon – I spotted his brakeless old bicycle leaning against the wall – when I went down with Heather to get some supplies. He soon had us both laughing at his latest anecdotes and, before he left, extracted a promise from Heather to come up and see them at Clydach before her stay was finished.

Having got some tinned 'steek', some 'Jackob's' biscuits and sundry other oddly pronounced items from old Uncle, together with an interesting cross-section of village gossip, we got back into the Old Girl with our spoils, and Heather was full of the idea of a trip up to Clydach.

'Surely you and I could go even if Bill won't come? It's only a couple of miles up that track according to Davey. And I'll bet they don't get many visitors, poor things, right up there on the mountainside. You've got to take me, and hang the farm jobs for one afternoon!'

And so I was prevailed upon to agree to a visit to the remote farm, something I should almost certainly never have done but for Heather's insistence and, as it turned out, something I should have been the poorer to have missed. Bill remained adamant that he couldn't spare the time, so we asked Mrs Lloyd Vaughan if she'd care to come with us, and the three of us eventually set out one sunny afternoon about a week later.

'It will be interesting to meet the elder brother, John,' said Mrs L.V. 'They say he hardly ever goes anywhere. A shy man I should think, unlike brother Davey. But everyone speaks well of him.'

We soon reached the river and crossed the footbridge near the little ford before starting to climb the steep track in search of

Clydach. It proved a long drag in the hot summer sun, and long before we reached the farm, we began to dream about Davey's 'dish of tea'. The thought came to me of the awful difficulties the brothers faced in getting supplies to their remote hide-out, for everything would have to be brought by horse and cart from the ford, and I suspected we didn't know we were born at Vendre by comparison with the problems they faced here.

After a good hour's uphill slog, with many rests to slow the progress, we eventually reached some farm buildings in a slight dell on the hillside. If Davey was at all put out to see the party of three, with the wife of the squire amongst us, he certainly didn't show it. He welcomed us as if he was doing it every day, chatting affably as he showed us the calves at great length. From the calves we moved on to admire the pigs and from the pigs to a batch of chicks, and when he ran out of animals to show us he went on chatting gaily in the yard.

We were all really rather flaked out after our long climb in the heat of the afternoon, and I began to fear that brother John must be out and we were going to get neither tea nor sit-down. But as I stood with faltering spirits I thought I saw something move in the corner of my eye, over near the house, some thirty yards from where we stood. The second time it happened I saw it clearly. What looked like a panful of sweepings was being ejected powerfully from a downstairs window. The unseen hand of John was evidently putting the house in order. So that's what we were waiting for!

After what seemed an eternity, with never a hint of embarrassment in his demeanour, Davey finally got round to what we were all hoping for and suggested, casually, that we might care for some tea. The Squire's wife looked as if she needed something stronger by this time, but we all accepted gratefully and moved towards the house.

The room, I noticed, was nicely furnished and showed no sign of recent activity in the way of tidying-up, while brother John received us with unruffled courtesy, his rather solemn manner giving no hint of anything amiss. He was a taller and slimmer man than Davey with greying hair and a fine strong face that exuded sincerity and dignity. We enjoyed a welcome tea, complete with cakes and biscuits, rather miraculously pro-duced, heard some amusing fishing stories and learnt a little about farming in their far-off situation. Mrs L.V. picked their brains a bit about the finer points of poultry rearing while Heather seemed fascinated by everything the brothers said. But the high point of the visit came after tea when we stopped to watch the milking, a very assorted bunch of cows having come into the yard of their own volition while we were having tea. I wondered which of the buildings was the cowshed but, as it turned out, there was no need of one; the brothers simply took a pail and stool apiece and moved round the yard, milking each cow in turn. Why the cows stood still, free as they were to wander off at will and with no attempt to bribe them with hay or cake as we did at Vendre, was more than I could understand. But stand still they did and the milker could operate in comparative comfort, with none of the heat and compression between bellies that we had to endure in our cowshed. Then I reflected that the TT milk production rules would scarcely have permitted this time-honoured system at Vendre, so much more natural and restful as it was. This milk was for stock-feeding only. Clydach being much too far from the road for them to sell to the Milk Marketing Board.

'They're quite the most marvellous pair

I've ever met!' sighed Heather, almost in tears, as we made our way back down the track.

We gathered somewhere along the line that they were sons of very respectable Welsh townspeople and had taken over Clydach some thirty years before. They must have been happy in their remote world, their expressions said it clearly enough, but I couldn't help feeling sad that they led such basic lives.

Chapter 27

Brinkmanship

Our second summer's haymaking proved a far more efficient process thanks to the hardware we'd acquired since the hayfork-and-taxi combination of the previous year. Caractacus chuffed around with the side-rake-cum-swath-turner to such good effect that the only fork-work called for was in making the haycocks and loading them on to the trailer. Not that we didn't have our little alarms and excursions with the outsize tractor and trailer combination in our steep fields and narrow gateways, but we somehow overcame them, even to the extent of taking three times as much hay per load up the steep track to the barn, and so speeding things up immeasurably. The only job for which we still had to rely on Kropje's tractor was the mowing, this being too delicate a task altogether for the cumbersome Caractacus if we weren't to damage half the crop. We repaid Kropje by lending him the big trailer to help with his own harvest and, indeed, it was on one of these occasions that the most memorable event of the year's haymaking took place.

Although Kropje never lost a chance of complaining about the size of our trailer, he always used it in preference to his own diminutive model, hitching it on to his little tractor like a tug with a giant oil tanker in tow. We were careful to limit the size of loads we built, more especially perhaps because of the nasty sunken lane which bordered the lower edge of his steep fields, rendering them a grade or two more dangerous than our own steep ones at Vendre. But it was while hauling one of these fields that Kropje came within a hair's breadth of hurtling over the sheer twelve-foot drop, tractor, trailer, load and all.

We had spent an entire afternoon bringing in the top half of one particular field, just the three of us, and the evening dew was beginning to dampen the grass as we struggled to get all the remaining hay on to the final load. It turned out to be a much larger load than we had previously taken, but the trip to the hay barn was fairly straightforward and we had no wish to return for another load.

It so happened that, as a result of grazing late in the spring, Kropje had left much of the lower half of the field uncut, and as he approached this longer grass, which we had safely traversed all day, Bill shouted from his high perch atop the load, 'I SHOULDN'T TAKE HER THROUGH THAT LONG GRASS WITH THE DEW ON IT!'

'VEEL BE ALL RIGHT!' sang back Kropje, with a cheery wave.

As Bill pointed out later, things might not have turned out so badly if Kropje had had the sense to steer directly down the steep slope. As it was, he continued to tack obliquely, so that once the grip of the tractor's rear wheels started to go he rapidly lost control. His second mistake was in standing on the brake, an action that achieved nothing by way of slowing up proceedings but a good deal in removing his last vestige of steering control.

With the load swaying perilously as it gathered speed, Bill decided to bale out, and a moment later landed at my feet as I was hurrying along behind. We could only watch, fascinated, as the careering combination headed for disaster, strewing hay to right and left, and swinging crazily from side to side. But, even as we held our breath for a spectacular plunge to the lane below, there came a frightful sound of grinding machinery, the trailer slewed round at right angles spilling half its load across the field, and the whole thing ground to a miraculous halt within a yard or two of the sheer drop. By some marvellous stroke of luck, the old mower had been lying innocently at the bottom of the field, the tractor had struck it amidships and locked with it to save the day.

'You all right, Kropje?' gasped Bill as we reached the scene and a pale and shaking Latvian emerged from behind the remnant of his load.

'I not afraid!' he stammered, unconvincingly. 'I am in many accidents and nussing can happen to me!'

The crop of peas and oats that we'd sown by hand in the autumn was coming on apace, but Bill was determined to get the hay safely brought in before making any start on the silage, which can be cut and carried in almost any weather since it goes straight into the pit in fresh condition without any drying out at all. Another factor weighing with us was that the later we left the cutting, the greater the bulk would be, an important consideration despite the falling off in feeding value that is supposed to result as the crop gets more mature, and coarser.

As things turned out, the weather, though starting off on the right foot that summer, rapidly deteriorated before we'd finished the hay. Our last field, indeed, was completely lost as depression followed depression to give nothing more than the single dry day on the 'ridge' between them. We made desperate attempts to dry it out, I remember, only to end up burning the black remains in early August. The Welsh weather was showing us just what it could do, and a frustrating experience it was.

The upshot of our hay troubles was that we didn't start on the big job of the silage till well into August, far too late in the season to achieve a good product according to the experts. The cutting and carting of the very heavy crop, which our peas and oats mixture had grown into in all the wet weather, proved a much heavier job than we'd anticipated, the peas having spread like tentacles to bind together in unwieldy masses and made doubly heavy by the water lying everywhere. Indeed, much of the job we did in driving rain, encumbered and uncomfortably over-heated by protective clothing as we were, even to the extent of the hated gumboots.

But all this we could shrug off as a weather hazard; it was in the matter of getting the heavy load into position alongside the pit that things really became difficult. This was something we hadn't foreseen, it never having entered our heads that we should be doing the job in a near-monsoon. The plan, from the first, had been to unload the silage from the top edge of the pit, thereby getting the obvious advantage of a downhill throw. Such was the situation of the pit that it had to be approached by tacking across a steep slope from the field gate some fifty yards away, something which Bill could have done with his eyes shut in normal conditions even having regard to the strange mounds and boggy patches that made the going so rough. To bring the heavy trailer neatly into position, with its lower wheel suitably close to the pit edge, was the sort of challenge Bill relished. But to achieve this delicate manoeuvre in progressively more slippery conditions as each load churned up its quota of mud, called for all Bill's nerve as well as skill.

The climax came one fearfully wet day, when having watched Bill perform yet another desperately risky approach, I almost wept in urging him to call it off until we got some dry weather. I suspect he put it down to my being an old woman once more, but the urgency of my appeal must have registered, for he agreed, rather to my surprise, to leave it for a bit, despite the knowledge that his precious silage would be adversely affected by doing so.

Eventually we finished the job in better conditions, the pit was filled well above its brim and the great heaps of earth all round were shovelled on top to seal it for the pickling process.

'So that's that till we open her up at Christmas!' sighed Bill, as we collected the tools, scarcely able to believe we had actually finished.

'What about the sample Morgan's going

to do? When will that be?'

'Probably about October,' returned Bill. 'It'll be interesting to hear what sort of quality it is after all that wet.'

My idea of fun was to get aboard the Old Girl and bumble off somewhere. Bill, generous-minded and above such pettiness himself, was always willing for me to do most of the car errands while he struggled on with some tedious routine work. Once a week, at a minimum, I would drive down to the village to replenish the groceries and get any items of animal feeding stuffs we happened to be short of.

'You'd better bring a bag of milk nuts to carry us over to Monday's delivery,' shouted Bill one afternoon as I was getting into the car.

The usual interminable session with Uncle culminated in my order for the bag of cow-cake.

'Indeed, there's only the one part-bag of cake left with me,' apologised the old man, 'but you are welcome to that one, whatever.'

We repaired to the garage, where such commodities were stored, and Uncle placed the half-empty sack on his old-fashioned scales, fiddled about with the sliding arm and announced it to be sixty-seven pounds, indeed.

'Now, let me see!' he began, scrawling a complicated sum on the whitewashed wall in an effort to arrive at the cost. 'Yes, that will be thirty-four and sixpence, now then!'

'Surely that's not right, Mr Thomas? A whole bag is less than two pounds, isn't it?'

'Drat! So it is, indeed,' agreed Uncle, starting a fresh sum on the wall. This time it came out to about twelve shillings, an equally ridiculous figure in the other direction, for I was getting more than half a bagful.

'Er … shall I have a go, Mr Thomas?' I suggested, taking over the pencil and producing a third set of figures on the wall. But by this time old Uncle was thoroughly demoralised and he accepted my honestly-arrived-at figure without question, though his manner seemed to say I was working a big fiddle which he was too generous-minded to quibble about.

Chapter 28

Binoculars at the Ready

Bill was determined to make up for the lack of cultivations we had been able to do at Vendre by re-seeding some of our old grass fields that autumn, now that we had an iron horse to do it with. He started going the rounds of the farm sales once again, and soon brought back a fine old three-furrow trailer plough, together with some harrows and a horse roller that had been adapted for hauling by a tractor, all securely lashed to the trailer with binder twine.

'Everyone says it'll be very difficult ploughing with Caractacus,' said Bill as we struggled to unload the trailer against a bank, 'but I can't really see why. And we should be able to manage without discs with Caractacus's weight and steel wheels to break up the furrows.'

Fortunately, the weather recovered its composure sufficiently for us to tackle the cultivations in reasonably dry conditions, and it was quite a thrill to be using our own equipment, even if I was kept busy unhitching the plough at the turns to save leaving excessively wide headlands to accommodate Caractacus's cumbersome sweep. It probably took us twice as long as it would have done with a normal tractor, even allowing for the extra furrow, but it was worth it to be getting the job done without hiring or borrowing, for a change. Our old friend, the fiddle, did all the sowing for us, coping very well with the small Italian Ryegrass seeds, and the fertilisers went on in the usual Vendre style as Bill and I marched and counter-marched till we were fit to drop. In all we re-seeded three fields, one of which was the six-acre that had just produced the silage crop. Two of the three were eligible for ploughing grants, this being a subsidy from the Ministry intended to encourage the fullest use of land, which cut the cost to us by about half and so made it eminently worthwhile, for there is no comparison between the lush growth of a new ley and the poor permanent grass of upland Wales.

As soon as all three fields were ready, rolled flat to give a professional appearance and conjuring up visions of fine crops blowing in the spring breeze, Bill 'phoned Morgan at the Ministry offices in Newtown, and not long afterwards the great man arrived to check that the work was to his satisfaction and to take a sample from the silage pit.

'A great pity it was cut so late,' he lamented when Bill told him of our hold-ups with the silage. 'The protein percentage will be badly affected, you see; too coarse for much feeding value. Pity! Pity!'

I walked down with them to inspect the fields, keen to hear what the expert had to say, but conscious of Morgan's superior glance and wondering if I should have touched my forelock when spoken to. He was rather like a provincial policeman, far too important to treat people with respect and reluctant to converse with riff-raff.

'What should the protein percentage be then?' I ventured.

He didn't deign to answer for some time, preferring perhaps to keep the conversational initiative himself, but in his own good time he got round to it:

'About 14% is average, higher when molasses is used. You'll be lucky if yours reaches 10% cutting it so late. Yes … pity, indeed!'

Morgan duly passed our cultivations and took the sample from the pit. A couple of weeks later, the laboratory report arrived: 'Protein content – 19.4%; Feeding Value – HIGH'. What a turn-up for the book! I was beside myself with delight and wondered how friend Morgan would get out of that one. It is good, indeed, to prove the experts wrong, especially when they are as smug as that one.

'See that rabbit?' hissed Bill one evening when we were enjoying a rare walk with the rifle.

'No. Where?'

CRACK!... 'There! Look, he's bowled over. Just below that ash.'

Trigger sped off to confirm his master's words as I glimpsed the bobbing white tail of the wounded bunny thrashing about in the shadows at the far end of the next hedge. How Bill could spot them sitting still almost in the next parish was more than I could understand, far less hit them with a 'two-two' slug at such a range. Even so, I was rather fascinated, and when Bill suggested I might care to take a walk with the rifle myself a few evenings later I thought it might be worth trying. I took the precaution, though, of grabbing an old pair of binoculars we had in the house, knowing I might otherwise see nothing at all if past experience was anything to go by.

'The far side of the three-cornered field is a good spot at this time of day,' advised Bill, as I was leaving. 'As you come up over the crest in the middle you'll probably find one or two grazing on the other slope.'

I had Trigger firmly by the lead and set off on a bit of a circular tour, down along the river bank and back up towards the field Bill had been talking about. I saw any number of rabbits with the binoculars on the way, but they all disappeared without trace as I tried to get within range. When, eventually, I approached the small crest in the three-cornered field, I had no way of knowing if there were any rabbits on the other side or not, so I crept as stealthily as possible, checking with the binoculars every few paces. Just as I reached the most critical point and was delicately raising the binoculars for a final peep, the evening stillness was shattered by a raucous guffaw from the direction of the lane, about two hundred yards away on my right.

'BAHNG!!' came a coarse female shout. 'BAHNG, BAHNG!', followed by peals of laughter which could only have one source of origin – by a cruel twist of fate Eirwen

234

Price was passing in the lane.

I was so mortified to be caught in such an unconventional sportsman's attitude, binoculars at the ready, that I continued stiffly on my line, ignoring the rude interruption as if I'd been stone deaf, and not deigning even to glance up from the chase. Several more loud repetitions of 'bahng!' emanated from the undeterred Eirwen and further gales of mirth, to make doubly sure no rabbit remained to be shot at. I suppose Eirwen's reaction, countrywoman that she was, was very natural, but it didn't do much for my budding interest in shooting; indeed, it put me off for good and I never ventured out with the gun again.

One other incident with the rifle happened at about this time. It was a Saturday afternoon and we'd just enjoyed a pleasant lunch of Maida's weekly pie. We planned to do some stake cutting up in the wood and Bill decided to bring the rifle along as rabbits often appeared in the field below when we were on that job.

We had scarcely got into the wood proper when Bill's sharp ears detected a dog some way further up.

'Poachers!' he hissed. 'Come on, let's try and catch them red-handed!' I wasn't too keen on the idea myself and would have preferred to let them poach on, whoever they were, but Bill had the fire of battle in his eyes.

'Blasted swine! I'll soon sort them out!' he grunted as he hurried on ahead in big farmer fashion.

The wood was exceedingly steep and soon Bill was some way in front. Suddenly, to my alarm, I saw him taking aim at something beyond and letting go with five rounds rapid. As the loud CRACKS of the rifle echoed deafeningly through the wood I ran hard to get up to where Bill stood.

'What the hell are you doing?' I gasped. 'Trying to kill someone?'

'Oh, it's all right. I was firing into a tree trunk above that dell,' said Bill. 'That's where they are, I'm sure. Come on, let's see!'

We reached the edge of the dell and peered over.

'Oh, Lord, it's Charlie!' gasped Bill, as he took in a small group huddled against a tree-stump.

'Sorry, Charlie, I didn't know it was you. Thought it was poachers from the village,' mumbled Bill, apologetically.

Poor Charlie was cowering with his little boy and a dog, obviously doing a spot of rabbiting. The boy was in tears and the skin-and-bones dog was visibly trembling at his feet.

"E's 'ad it worse than what we 'ave!' was Charlie's only remark, pointing to the hound.

With one or two more weak apologies from Bill we took our leave, wondering if we'd made a life-long enemy of our neighbour. This would be a serious matter if it were so, for we knew from several sources that Charlie was a cantankerous fellow, and we feared the worst. But, happily, he didn't seem to bear us any grudge over the incident, and never alluded to it again.

As Christmas approached once more, we sat down to another vast 'financial'. So pleased were we to find that we really had turned the corner during the year, to become a viable business, that we decided to celebrate by booking ourselves into a hotel in Newtown for Christmas dinner. After a very early evening milking, we duly motored over to join the festivities at the 'Angel', the best hotel in those parts and with a reputation for a bit more life than most Welsh hotels can claim. We were keeping our fingers crossed that the forecast of snow would not materialise and were relieved to find nothing worse than a heavily overcast sky when we eventually clambered into the Old Girl for the trip home. It had been a good evening, though girl-less as usual, and we had made the most of the food and wine. Bill took the wheel and soon clicked into his Mr Toad role on the empty roads as we bumbled lightheartedly through the dark night.

We had just passed through the large village of Llanfair, with a dozen miles or so still to go, when the car started to play up, recovered a few times and finally spluttered to a halt. The petrol meter had long since ceased to work on the old taxi, our standard method of checking being the use of a stick we carried specially for sounding the tank, but we quickly guessed that to be the trouble and sat wondering where on earth to get some juice at that hour of the night. Bill instinctively switched off the headlights while we discussed the problem, but inadvertently put out the side-lights at the same time, one further click on the same switch.

As we sat pondering in the darkness of the deserted country road we felt a sudden jolt, followed by a frightful clatter behind. We leapt out to find an elderly cyclist picking himself up in dazed fashion, clearly a bit the worse for the festive season.

'You didn't 'ave no lights, guv!' grumbled the old chap as we struggled to straighten out the handlebars of his bicycle.

'Neither did you!' retorted Bill, quick to head off any legal complications.

With that our friend re-mounted shakily and wobbled off into the darkness. Fortunately for us we found the people still up at the first house along the road and were able to borrow a can of petrol to get us home.

Chapter 29

This Blighted Farming

'I don't want to frighten you boys,' said Lewis the Vet ominously one night, squatting on his haunches in the pig-pen and playing his torch beam on a worried-looking porker we'd asked him to come to see, 'but I think we might have a case of anthrax by here!'

Anthrax! That's all we need, I thought. First we give up our entire lives to this blighted farming, slaving away to all hours in rain and muck, sacrificing all civilised pleasures and social life, then find ourselves forced to take risks which could bring us to the grave itself at any moment, and now – to cap it all – the dreaded anthrax. In my ignorance of farming matters I equated it with foot-and-mouth disease, picturing our precious animals piled up for burning and the end of our farming enterprise. And, to make it worse, I didn't know to what extent we were, ourselves, at risk.

'I can't be sure about it. We'll have to wait till morning,' Lewis went on. 'Nothing you can do now but leave him where he is.'

Of all the shocks we had at Vendre this was the most dramatic, if only for the dire consequences the diagnosis entailed. Bill was able to reassure me on the mass slaughter prospect, though it would mean burning the carcass, police involvement and heaven knows what. We knew Lewis to be an excellent vet with a reputation second to none in those parts, and it seemed hardly likely that he'd suspect anthrax without good cause, but there was nothing we could do about it, so we shrugged our shoulders and left it in the lap of the gods. But we did feel a bit like condemned men that night.

The porker was very much alive when we looked at him first thing next morning and our spirits rose. When Lewis called soon after breakfast the anticlimax was completed by the information that, not only was the anthrax a false alarm, but there was nothing whatsoever the matter with the pig. If he realised the effect his fears had had on Bill and me, he certainly didn't give any indication of it.

'Nothing wrong with 'im!' he declared in a matter-of-fact tone, after a thorough examination. 'Hot water, soap and towel!'

This escape certainly did something to give us renewed energy for all the routine work we were, by this time, struggling to get through in the hours of daylight. Quite apart from the twice-daily Sorcerer's Apprentice act with the whey buckets, now augmented with a good deal of meal for the sixty or so pigs in various stages of growth, we had, every day, to cut and carry some quarter ton of hay, feed the young and dry stock, muck out cowshed and pig-pens, and from Christmas onwards cut and cart the heavy silage, to say nothing of the major task of milking night and morning. All this routine work left little time for doing anything extra and I began to see why the small farmer is often likened to a slave in his seven-day week of animal tending. Of course, even in winter it has its compensations: it is varied work, it is satisfying, it is constructive and, above all perhaps, the farmer is his own boss, able to do things his own way without any pressures from above. Bill, spurred on by the worthwhile aspects of the job, never seemed to grumble, but that winter my own moral stamina began to falter at the incessant grind.

I had never come into close contact with silage before. Getting a whiff of the stuff on passing some farm, I'd often imagined it to be a foul-smelling substance that cows must be mad to eat. But, strangely, the pungent smell seems to diminish as one gets closer, and good silage, pickled as it is to a dark green substance scarcely recognisable as the original crop, has a pleasant, almost sweet, smell at close range. Certainly the cows relish it, for it is virtually fresh food for them at a time when nothing is growing in the fields. They loved our peas and oats mixture, that I can vouch for, and we saw the milk yields go up with a bang from the moment we opened the pit.

We never needed to cut and carry kale after that first year when our efforts at singling it had resulted in giant plants. Subsequently we simply broadcast the seed and grazed the crop in strips with the electric fence. Root crops we grew every year, mainly swedes, and fed them in small quantities right through the winter to augment the kale and silage. I remember being fascinated at the way in which a cow can demolish a nine-inch swede in a few bites. The technique is to corner the big vegetable in her manger and then apply her sharp lower jaw like a scoop, using the toothless upper jaw simply to hold it with. By putting her weight behind the operation, great slices are prised off and the swede demolished in no time. Smaller vegetables, though, including uncut potatoes, are dangerous to cows, which can choke in trying to swallow them whole. It always struck me as a strange combination that a cow should be so very particular about what she will eat, thanks to her delicate sense of smell, and yet have a mouth of such insensitivity that she can chew up the most frightful thistles and other rough fodder with relish.

About this time, and in consequence, probably, of the greatly increased stocks of feeding stuffs we were storing for our expanding livestock, we began to find rats everywhere, whereas previously it had been only mice.

One morning when Bill had gone off

somewhere, I was occupied at my old job of mucking out and, incidentally, going through a rare patch of depression at what life had brought me to, there being no prospect that I could see of our ever being able to afford a better farm, when I caught a glimpse through the cowshed door of one of our hens running round the yard in figures of eight. On taking a proper look I was astonished to see a huge rat not far behind, something I had never heard of but which Bill later assured me was by no means unusual. I dashed out in a vain attempt to clobber the rat with the broom I was holding, but succeeded only in causing it to lope off and disappear into a nearby wall.

Not long after that little episode, Bill and I were enjoying a Sunday sit-down by the fire when another cat-sized rat walked casually across the kitchen from one door to the other, as if it owned the place. We were both so surprised we just watched it go.

'Right, that's it!' said Bill. 'They say that once you see them in the house, the farm is really infested. I'll get some poison tomorrow.'

So we set about destroying them in earnest, and during the next week or two we found dozens of the brutes hunched up, dying, in the buildings as the poison did its horrid work. According to the tins, the stuff contained phosphorus and, for all my dislike of rats, it worried me that they should die such an agonising death. Why couldn't science produce something more humane, I wondered; presumably for the usual reason of economy.

Another little hazard that our friends the hens had to face that winter was that their favourite roosting-place, on the beams of one of the barns, had recently been pressed into service as an overflow pig-pen. Why the silly birds should occasionally fall off their safe perches was something neither of us could understand, unless the porkers were able to mesmerise them in the dark, but from time to time we would hear a frightful squawking to denote just such an event. The first few times it happened we rushed up in a rescue attempt, only to find very little evidence beyond a satisfied expression on the porkers' faces and the odd feather in their chops. Undoubtedly the deaths were short, if hardly sweet. To counter these sad losses we did what we could to stop them roosting there, even spending many a difficult hour removing them after they'd gone to roost, by which time they were several stages dafter than usual, which is saying a lot with chickens.

The event that finally decided Bill he'd had enough of them was what came to be known in Vendre's history as 'Trigger's egg-feed'. We staggered in for a reviving bite to eat one evening, after a tough session with the work and the elements, to find the kitchen floor strewn right across with egg-shells and Trigger lying under the table in a bloated condition. Once again we had failed to latch the outer door and Trigger had scoffed about three dozen precious eggs all ready washed and graded for sale. This was the last straw in Bill's eyes, what with the deaths by violence, the poor price we got for the eggs, and the time taken in gathering and washing the things. He decided the time had come to redeem his bit of capital and the remaining forty or so found their way to the local butcher, via Bill's skilful neck-pulling, a trick I had no wish to learn. The truth was that they had done us very well but were now past their prime and hardly worth the keeping. Even so, it was sad to see them go, for we knew many by name and they had been with us from the start. The place would never be quite the same again but, as Bill often tried to tell me, 'There's no place for sentiment in farming', an old adage I always found hard to accept.

When the weather was really cold, with the bedroom like an ice-box, Bill and I would go for weeks without undressing for bed. Boots and jackets would be discarded, windows jammed shut, and we'd submerge beneath our respective bedclothes like Eskimos in the freezing igloo.

One night I had just floated off into blessed dreamland when a loud crash brought me back with a jerk.

'What the hell was that?' I blurted out, surfacing, but no reply came from Bill whose steady breathing showed he hadn't heard it. 'Strange,' I thought, 'and he's such a light sleeper, usually. Must be dead beat, I suppose.'

The following night much the same thing happened, only this time it was a double crash that wrecked my slumbers.

'Bill! BILL! Didn't you hear that?' I shouted, wishing I had some matches handy.

'What are you talking about?' came Bill's sleepy voice. 'I didn't hear anything. You must have dreamt it!'

On the third night I was awakened by the

father and mother of all bumps in the night. Not one or two crashes this time but a room-shaking succession of at least twenty, merging into one almighty crescendo, right alongside my bed. I sat bolt upright, convinced I was back in my service days and the Germans had got through at last. Only then did I detect a muffled laugh from my 'sleeping' partner.

'If that doesn't stop you snoring, nothing will!' came Bill's voice from the dark.

'Snoring? Me? I don't believe it!' I croaked, weakly.

'You don't imagine I brought that sack of swedes up here for nothing, do you?'

'Swedes! Was that what made all that row, you swine?'

'Well, my boots didn't do much good the last couple of nights, so I had to try something a bit stronger,' he chuckled. 'You were snoring like a grampus so, for Gawd's sake, lie on your side or something. I never heard such a din!'

So that was it. Those crashes last night and the night before were his massive boots being lobbed in the air, and now he'd gone and emptied a sack of swedes by my bed! Some people have a strange sense of humour, I thought, ruefully. Enough to give a bloke heart failure.

I decided to get over on my side without delay, and stay there.

Chapter 30

A Nice Bit of Ham to Taste

As the drying winds of March did their vital work to enable the stock to return to the fields once more, and the days lengthened to remove the awful pressure of so much routine work having to be squeezed in between breakfast and tea-time, Bill and I were able to turn our minds to other things than sheer survival. This is the time of year, as the countryside begins to stir from its winter torpor, when the farmer's plans must be laid for the ensuing year, crops decided on and preparations put in hand for the hectic outdoor days ahead. But, as our third Lady Day at Vendre approached, one thought loomed above all others: it was time to take action on the next step of the master plan. We were now established with the nucleus of a dairy herd and further expansion of stock would be impossible after this year on the little farm. If we didn't move to better pastures before the year was out we should find ourselves having to mark time, and that would never do. Consequently we undertook a long search over on the better land towards the English border, and in Shropshire itself, for the combination of substantial house and land that we sought. Suffice it to say that we made several unsuccessful sorties to those parts before coming to the conclusion that what we looked for was unobtainable and likely to be way beyond our limited finances even if we could find it. Fine country houses going begging there certainly were, as I had been led to believe, but what we were not aware of before then was that the land belonging to them had invariably been let off to the neighbouring farmer as an act of patriotism during the war, and was now irrecoverable. It was a scandal, of course, on a par with what happened to people who responded to the country's need by putting their savings into War Loan, only to find that it dwindled after the war. The Government, by way perhaps of showing the country's gratitude to those who had responded to the call for land, had subsequently brought in the

Security of Tenure Act to ensure that the owner couldn't get his land back, even when he wanted to sell up.

There was only one thing for it if we were to continue with our plans: to turn our sights westward to the lowlands beyond Snowdonia, to the Lleyn peninsula sticking out to the north of Cardigan Bay where, rumour had it, prices were very different and chances of finding what we wanted rather better. I realised only too well that prospects of getting pupils for my proposed school must be far less promising in an area so far from the centres of population but, as the idea was to have boarders only, it by no means ruled the scheme out. So over the mountains we bumbled in the Old Girl, through the great passes and down the wide sweep to the sea at Portmadoc.

As things turned out, the 'master plan' of building a school on the back of the established farm, never did come to pass, thanks to the continuing problem of the Security of Tenure laws. Bill, however, found the farm he wanted, at a price he could afford, to carry on the farming enterprise and, subsequently, I was able to lease a fine property for my school in a pretty seaside resort not too far from the farm. But the prospect of an end, at last, to our days of peasant farming came as a badly-needed shot in the arm to me, for my moral stamina, unlike Bill's, was wearing mighty thin at the edges.

I determined to enjoy the remaining months at Vendre till Michaelmas, when we were to take over the new place, and I soon found myself appreciating once more the charms of the little farmstead which had faded somewhat over the years. I had enjoyed so much of the worthwhile life, but the daily slog of routine work, more especially in wet weather, had stretched me to the limits.

When we told Maida Granitt the news, she decided to have the first spring-clean the little house had known in our time there, and Bill and I were ordered to lend a hand with moving carpets and heavy furniture.

When the inside of the little house was finished we started on the outside and white-washed the walls till it looked to be made of icing sugar. The cowshed came in for the same treatment and so did most of the outbuildings, so that the little farmstead looked prettier that spring, nestling into its valley side of green fields and woods, than it had ever done and I could see it was going to be a wrench to leave it after all.

I had almost forgotten by this time, about the pig Evans-the-Road had had for fattening on scrap the previous spring, but stopping me one day on a visit to old Uncle at the shop, he told me to call in to see the pig next time I was down there of an evening. Considering he'd had it for over a year I suppose I should have expected something of a transformation from the fifteen-inch weaner we had handed over, but I was in no way prepared for the veritable monster that Evans proudly introduced me to when I duly called later that week.

'There now! How's that for feeding?' purred the old boy as I got my first view of the grossest animal I'd ever seen, resembling a small barrage balloon and looked, for all the world, as if it had been inflated by a pressure pump. I had no need to make polite comments – my stunned silence was eloquence itself, for unlike our own porkers which left us for the chop at about twenty weeks, this one was at least as long as its mother, Gertie, and about five times as broad, with its back wide and flat enough to lay the table on and very different from the lean shape of the sows. It seemed to me that Evans had enough meat there to feed the entire village rather than just his own bachelor establishment.

'A couple of weeks more I'll give him!' smirked Evans, going into his chop-licking routine once more. 'And there'll be a bit to taste for you and your brother later on when it's all cured.'

I hate to think of the dreadful business of Evan's actual slaughtering, done in the time-honoured fashion of cutting its throat on a bench and letting it bleed to death, scream-ing, surely one of the most barbaric of human institutions and enough to put any sensitive person off meat for ever, but I have to confess I didn't hesitate to sample the ham when it finally arrived some six weeks later. Nor can I deny that it was far and away the tastiest piece of ham I have ever eaten, the expert curing having achieved a flavour one never gets from the shop variety. And I appreciated at last, why Evans always licked his lips so pointedly when making any refer-ence to his pig.

Chapter 31

The Thunderstorm Field

For our final summer's haymaking at Vendre we made a further big advance by getting the hay baled by a contractor, thereby cutting down a good deal on the risk of losing it to the elements, of which we'd had a nasty experience the previous year, and at the same time eliminating a lot of the hard labour associated with handling loose hay. The contractor charged sixpence a bale, I remember, at that time and Gareth reckoned we had taken leave of our senses to waste good money, but we decided it was worth it now that it was no longer necessary to save every penny.

But the advance was not without its drawbacks, for perhaps nowhere more than in rural Wales, the wink and the nod of old acquaintance plays its part. The man who did the baling was as susceptible as most other countryfolk with the result that, however clear the understanding that he would come to you on a particular day, there was never any guarantee that it would be at a convenient time. In fact, if the day in question turned out to be ideal baling weather, he could be stopped all along his route and, in Wales, there is no such thing as a refusal to an urgent request amongst farming folk. The result was that, while preparing for the baler's arrival as soon as the dew was off the grass of a morning, one often waited half the day before the man arrived.

The most striking example of this, a day that put years on both of us, concerned the field of hay which came to be known in Vendre's annals as 'The Thunderstorm Field'. We had spent the usual week or so in bringing a fine crop to the point of readiness for baling and the day dawned fine and sunny, just what the doctor ordered for completing the job and getting it safely into the barn. The hay was at the ideal point in the delicate process of 'making', and our spirits soared as we walked the field that morning in glorious sunshine, savouring the scent of handfuls wherever we chose to sample it.

'It really is a bit of good stuff this time!' said Bill a dozen times. 'Just look at the green in it; real feeding value in that, you know.'

We were disappointed, but not despondent

when lunch-time came with no sign of the baler. But, as the afternoon wore on, the sun gradually became hazy until, by tea-time, clouds were beginning to bank up ominously in the distance. It was obvious we were heading for a thunderstorm as we waited with increasing anxiety for the sound of the baler in the lane, but time wore steadily on, lightning began to play around some of the blacker cloud-banks, and still no baler. We guessed what had happened: other farmers seeing the threatening storm clouds, must have side-tracked our baler, and we could only wait and pray he'd reach us in time to save the perfect crop.

By seven o'clock, things were looking frightful, with great 'anvils' building up all round as several storms seemed to be converging right above to crush us. Then, as the first heavy drops started to fall, the baler came trundling round the corner of the lane.

'Duw, Duw, anwyl! I hope I'm not too late, whatever!' gasped the tough Welshman, glancing at the sky as he swung his baler through the narrow gateway. I couldn't help a surge of admiration as he started off along the rows of hay at full throttle, about three times the normal rate with engine screaming. You must hand it to a Welshman when circumstances call for desperate measures; their sense of the dramatic will always ensure that they rise to the occasion. I would have thought twice about the risk of taking the machine into the field at all, with so much forked lightning about, but not he, and the baler was thumping round the field at prodigious speed as Bill dashed to get the trailer for picking up the bales.

No sooner had we started to load the trailer, than the Welshman shouted he'd be needing more twine, so I was despatched to get some from Watkyn post haste, and with things looking black in more than one sense I shot off up the lane in the Old Girl, leaving Bill frantically loading bales on his own in what seemed to me the dying moments of our precious field of hay.

When I drew up at Watkyn's, in something of a flap owing to the urgency of the situation, the old chap was staring, open-mouthed at the fireworks of the storm.

'Diawl! Look at that 'un!' he whistled, while I did my best to urge him to produce some baler twine. 'And there's another bugger for you! Whew!'

It took several valuable minutes, with him pulling his most comical faces and uttering a variety of ejaculations, before he condescended to give me the twine, and all the time I knew the hay was hanging in the balance. Watkyn was showing, once again, his refusal to be pressurised, but I knew it would be fatal to lose patience and eventually he produced the goods to set me on my way.

By the time I got back the skies had blackened still further and torrential rain was sweeping down on all sides, but still, miraculously, it hadn't burst on Vendre. To cap everything, it had become extraordinarily oppressive, so that Bill and I were pouring with sweat as we strained every sinew to save as many bales as possible from the inevitable cloudburst.

But that cloudburst never came. Gradually the threat diminished and the hay was carted almost unscathed, albeit at great cost in sweat and effort. We learnt next day that Pen-y-bont, barely three miles from us, had been almost washed away, and several villages in the vicinity had chalked up a record rainfall. It was the nearest thing to a miracle we ever experienced at Vendre.

Another little drama that caught up with us in the middle of our final summer concerned a small field near the house which we had sown to kale earlier in the year. If anyone had told me, prior to that experience, that it was possible actually to hear a crop being consumed by caterpillars, I should have put it in the category of tall stories. But that is exactly what befell our two acres or so of kale in early July of that dry summer, by which time the plants were a foot or so high with wide green leaves.

For a few days we had noticed an unusual number of white butterflies flitting about over the crop, and soon afterwards every leaf was plastered with caterpillars. So, come to that, was everything leafy on the farm, as well as all metal objects and even many of the walls of the buildings. Standing at the edge of the kale field, the sound of tiny bits of leaf dropping on the dry ground was clearly audible as the grubs stripped them steadily bare.

By the time we managed to borrow spraying equipment and set about trying to apply the chemical thoroughly to the undersides of the leaves, many of them weren't worth saving, having been reduced to gossamer-like skeletons of what they had been a few days earlier. It had been a veritable plague and brought home to us something of what it must be like to lose your crops to a plague of locusts, but fortunately we were not very dependent on the kale that year as we planned to move farm in the autumn and would simply have used it as supplementary grazing in September.

Casting my mind back over the years to the light-hearted days at Vendre Fach, I recall numerous small happenings divorced now from the contexts in which they occurred. How, for example, did I come to pay a visit one evening to Bryncoed to find Gareth and Eirwen sitting in front of a fine wood-fire with no other light in the house at all? Perhaps they always economised in this fashion, for neither Bill nor I ever saw an oil-lamp anywhere on any of our visits. It was on this occasion that Eirwen told me the story of how she had first brought Gareth to meet her parents and get their approval. Evidently her father had been a tough old character of few words, and by way of testing the young man's eligibility, he produced from his pocket a six-inch nail, bent it into a horse-shoe shape and handed it to Gareth without a word. Gareth, who was nothing if not muscular, promptly straightened the nail and handed it back, thereby passing the old man's test with flying colours, for straightening the nail calls for even more strength than bending it, I'm told.

So many other snatches of life at Vendre

crowd in on my recollections – from topping and tailing roots in frosty weathers without gloves, naturally, to teaching baby calves to drink from a bucket, pleasant enough except when one's fingers touch the razor-sharp teeth at the back of the jaw that I would be hard put to it to list a fraction of them. But I still look back on those three years as a fine thing to have done and possibly the most worthwhile experience I've known. I count myself fortunate to have discovered, before it was too late, that life in the country, even at subsistence level, is preferable to the rush and artificiality of urban existence; let the high-pressure businessman or, come to that, the strike-happy industrial worker, have his big salary. He deserves it, deprived as he is of the soothing effects of living near to Nature. Give me the wonderful scents of the countryside, the balmy effect of sunshine on the rural scene and, above all, the sense of peace that comes from having no so-called 'superior' breathing down your neck.

Chapter 32

Fame at the Last

I doubt if Elsie the sow, in her wildest flights of imagination as she brought up her endlessly recurring families of piglets, ever dreamt that she might one day get her picture in the papers, far less feature in a magazine with world-wide coverage. But such proved to be the case, for it chanced that a photographic team promoting tourism in Britain happened to be doing mid-Wales that summer and had driven down our pretty lane to see what it had to offer.

Bill and I were enjoying an after-lunch pipe, prior to emerging once more for the afternoon's work, when I spotted through the kitchen window something I'd almost ceased to believe in: a beautiful girl picking her way through the hazards towards the front door.

Wondering if the pressures of Vendre were beginning to cause hallucinations, I hurried to open the door to our unlikely visitor.

'I'm frightfully sorry to disturb you,' she

began, with a smile that made me feel weak at the knees, 'but may we take a few photos of your farm? It's so pretty here and it wouldn't take us long.'

'Yes, of course, d-delighted,' I stammered, suddenly feeling conscious of my torn jacket and filthy trousers while a couple of men with photographic equipment approached from the front gate. It wasn't till later that we appreciated the shrewdness of the men in getting their breathtaking accomplice to call first; very few farmers could have said no to that young lady, and Bill and I almost fell over one another in our efforts to oblige.

'Would you like a calf or two to add colour?' suggested Bill.

'Oh, yes. A few animals would be a great help,' said the photographer, who was also the boss of the little party.

The girl was soon in raptures at the pretty little calves that Bill let out into the yard, but when the monstrous Elsie suddenly arrived unannounced in our midst the effeminate male model hopped with amazing alacrity on to the nearby trailer. It wasn't until Bill had scratched the sow's ear and given other assurances as to her tameness that the model, who represented the male half of the 'tourist couple' in the photographs, could be persuaded to return to ground level. The poor chap looked as if he had never left the city in his life and here he was being introduced to the horrific Elsie at close quarters.

In the course of the ensuing half-hour a score or so of photographs were taken in professional fashion, Bill and I being roped into most of them while the 'tourist couple' held hands and looked suitably impressed. Elsie, the calves and the quaint little house were given star billing, Bill was persuaded to pose with his twelve-bore gun and I to lean on a muck fork in true farmhand manner. With that girl watching I could have been prevailed upon to stand on my head in the midden, or anything else they may have wished.

But it was all over far too quickly and they moved on without even stopping for a cup of tea. Bill and I were left to ponder on what we were missing in our self-inflicted banishment from civilisation but, as often happens when one so much as catches sight of a really attractive girl, it did our morale good by confirming that such creatures did exist.

Before they left, the little group promised to send us any photos that might be used for publication, but as we gathered they were taking hundreds every day of a fortnight's tour, we rated our chances pretty slim. There hadn't even been any mention of payment for photos used, which we thought a bit thick, and we decided we'd probably hear no more.

Whether it was Elsie's smiling face that did the trick or the rustic attraction of the scene we never knew, but about half-way through September, when we were much preoccupied with our farm-moving preparations, a copy of the 'Come to Britain' tourist magazine arrived with a double-page spread given to Vendre under the heading 'OLD WELSH LONGHOUSE NEAR TRESILIOG'. There was Elsie, as large as life, and there was Bill's massive frame quite filling the front door where he'd been stationed with his twelve-bore. There was my torn jacket for all the world to see, and there were the little Ayrshire calves enjoying the attentions of the pretty model. Even Trigger had been captured perfectly by the expert cameraman, and his shots of the house with its steep backdrop of woods and fields knocked spots off the few photos we had already got of it. There was still no mention of any fees payable, which seemed hardly right to our farmers' way of thinking, but we were delighted to have the magazine and felt it was better than any payment.

Nor was that an end to the matter, for we were staggered to find a full-colour enlargement of the muck-fork-leaning scene appear as the mid-summer picture of the following year's Esso calendar, widely circulated in Wales. We were famous!

The last lap at Vendre was upon us. All plans regarding the big move had been completed and we were due to vacate on September 29th, the Michaelmas quarter day. As the time approached we both felt a real sadness to be leaving the quaint little farmstead which had been our home for the past three years, and we knew we would miss all the good friends we'd made amongst the neighbours. On the other hand, we felt we'd spent long enough in the wilderness, cut off from so much of what we had always been used to, and the prospect of returning to some of the more civilised pursuits of former days was good indeed, to say nothing of proper plumbing, electric light and drains, which we never got a whiff of in those outlandish parts. But we were conscious, too, of a pleasant sense of satisfaction at having achieved what we had set out to do in getting firmly established in the farming world, despite the hardships and the grind.

When the great day arrived at last, a small armada of vehicles was drawn up on the Vendre yard; a pantechnicon for the furniture, two large cattle trucks for all the animals and another lorry for the farm equipment. During the loading many of the neighbours put in an appearance to wish us well and lend a hand where needed.

First to arrive were Gareth and Eirwen.

'We've brought you a few loaves to help you settle in,' said Eirwen, handing over a bag of her delicious home-made bread. 'Mind how you go, now, and don't eat them all at once, will you?' she shrieked, splitting her sides at her own joke, as usual. We had finally solved Gareth's dilemma about what sort of tractor to buy by letting him have Caractacus for a song, having sadly realised the old tractor wouldn't be much good to us at the new place, quite apart from the problem of getting it there.

Davey Clydach arrived on his bike with a brace of pheasants as a parting gift– 'Best not let the Captain see them, isn't it?' he winked as he handed them over, hidden in a carrier bag – and Evans-the-Road thought we might like a piece more ham. Even old Uncle the Shop looked in to say goodbye. 'Always gentlemen!' he said, rather cryptically, and repeated it once or twice with a few 'indeeds' and 'whatevers' for good measure. Maida Granitt, who had done so much to save our reason in her weekly visits, was openly weeping while fat Ifor, whose lorries they were, was loading the livestock with great aplomb, still dressed to kill.

Kropje arrived, all smiles, on his little tractor and with no sign of the aggressiveness he usually showed.

'Veel be better next year!' he replied to Bill's good wishes. 'Zis vinter I make ze new range of buildings!'

Watkyn, who had come to supervise the loading of the heavy equipment, was swearing at everyone, and the old Captain turned up with Mrs L.V. in time to see us off.

'Well, there w'are, there w'are, old boy! That's life for you. The moving finger writes, and all that sort of thing, eh?'

'I think you've both been quite heroic,' said Mrs Lloyd-Vaughan, 'and you deserve a really good farm after this lot. Mind you come back and see us soon!'

One by one the lorries eased out of the gate and bumped off up the lane, the cows bellowing at the indignity of their incarceration and our colourful friends waving goodbye as Bill and I brought up the rear in the packed taxi.

Once on the road proper we sped past the convoy with our minds on a celebration beer at the pub in Llangynog, badly needed after the exertions of the morning, and, soon ensconced in the dark little smoke-room of 'The Black', as the pub was generally known – all pubs in those parts being 'Lions' of one colour or another – Bill held up his brimming tankard.

'Here's to our new neighbours!' he grinned, 'and if they're half as genuine as the ones we're leaving, we'll be fortunate.'

'Ah, well, here's hoping!' I said, sinking most of my beer at one draught as Bill did the same.

'I don't think we forgot anything in all that rush, do you?'

'No, I reckon we managed the lot,' I replied. 'What a job, though – I wouldn't like to move farm very often, I must say!'

'Oh, Lord!' spluttered Bill, draining his glass. 'I've just thought of something. We forgot to empty Johann Sebastian, and he was full to the brim!'

The hilarious vision conjured up of the dignified old Captain staggering up the Vendre path to empty the awful present we had inadvertently left him reduced us both to a state of near collapse, and so the Vendre story ended where it had so often been, on a note of coarse humour.

The publishers hope that this book has given you enjoyable reading. Large Print Books are especially designed to be as easy to see and hold as possible. If you wish a complete list of our books please ask at your local library or write directly to:

Dales Large Print Books
Magna House, Long Preston,
Skipton, North Yorkshire.
BD23 4ND

This Large Print Book, for people
who cannot read normal print,
is published under the auspices of

THE ULVERSCROFT FOUNDATION

... we hope you have enjoyed this book.
Please think for a moment about those
who have worse eyesight than you ...
and are unable to even read or enjoy
Large Print without great difficulty.

You can help them by sending a
donation, large or small, to:

**The Ulverscroft Foundation,
1, The Green, Bradgate Road,
Anstey, Leicestershire, LE7 7FU,
England.**
or request a copy of our brochure for
more details.

The Foundation will use all donations
to assist those people who are visually
impaired and need special attention
with medical research, diagnosis
and treatment.

Thank you very much for your help.